Endorsements:

"O'Connell speaks for all misfits and orphans everywhere. He has a stethoscopic ear for the sounds disappointment can squeeze from a human heart."
--W.A. Cole, *Book Reviewer, Cape Cod*

"Books have been written and movies created in the U.S. and Ireland reporting how children have been abused in orphanages. Tom O'Connell, author of *Call Me An Orphan: My Life as a Misfit*, exposes the pain and shame of an orphan abandoned by his living parents.

"In his psychological memoir, Tom reports how he was forced to live for nine years, from age 5 to 14, with five other boys in a similar discarded condition. They were placed at 'Mrs. White's house' by Catholic Charitable Bureau of the Archdiocese of Boston.

"Mrs. White, a violent perfectionist Irish widow, is a fierce 'guardian' who imposes her 'reign of terror' over her six young men. At age 14 he is set free to live with his lackadaisical Irish grandmother and neglectful father.

"Like a soldier returning from military service suffering from PTSD, Tom was a shy introverted boy who felt like a total misfit in the care of Mrs. White and later with his grandmother. His honest reporting on the painful, lonely journey, from age five to adulthood, draws the reader in to want to reach this lonely soul, affirming him as author, journalist, and decent human being."
--Dr. Finbarr Corr, *Psychotherapist, Author, former Priest, Educator*

Comments on Tom O'Connell's Books and Lectures

"Tom O'Connell connects with readers soul to soul...inspires...Tom's memoirs are written like novels."
--Jordan Rich, *WBZ News Radio 1030,* Boston

"It's the finest example of anyone writing on this subject."
--Don LaTulippe, *WPLM Radio*, Plymouth

"Your talk was warm and funny...You are a natural storyteller."
--Shirley Eastman, *Friends of the Cotuit Library*

"A page turner...mind boggling...a stunning view."
--Melora North, *Cape Cod Magazine*

"O'Connell writes compellingly."
--Melanie Lauwers, *Cape Cod Times*

"Thank you for your delightful presentation."
--Justine Bowen, *Irish American Club of Cape Cod*

"Very vivid...A fascinating read."
--Bob Silverberg, *Books & The World TV*

"Thank you for your delightful presentation...warmly received."
--Kathie Glynn, *Falmouth Public Library*

"Earthy dialogue sprinkled with wit, candor and affection." --*The Dedham Times*

Quotes from the pages of

Call Me An Orphan:

My Life as a Misfit~

A Psychological Memoir

by Tom O'Connell

(Chapter 1) I think the group of us boys at Mrs. White's house could have been accurately described as "displaced persons suffering from PTSD."

(Chapter 2) After my brother's death I continued to live in temporary care situations. And I had a screaming and crying fit each time I was relocated. I was not accepting what life was delivering to me. So I let the world know it.

(Chapter 3) I am speaking for myself, not other orphans, but for me there was never a healthy long term adjustment to my orphaned fate. At times I denied its impact on me. At other times I seldom thought about it. But its power has hovered in my psyche throughout my life.

(Chapter 4) As a female version of Captain Ahab, every detail of the ship Mrs. White controlled at 42 Mountain Avenue in Norwood was subject to her scrutiny. Also, being a complex personality, she was her own fiercely independent white whale as well as Captain of her own vessel.

(Chapter 6) I was always haunted by questions: "Why did God allow me to be uprooted from the only family I had ever felt comfortable with?" "Why did God let my only brother die?" "Why did I have to be a motherless kid?"

(Chapter 7) As for my father, I simply did not enjoy his company. I was always edgy around him, living with a state of high alertness. The deep wounds he had left on my spirit were inoperable. So living in his shadow on a daily basis was an ongoing psychological endurance test for me.

(Chapter 8) My balance was off and I had frequent dizzy spells. I had vertigo. I had asthmatic breathing difficulties. My blood pressure rose to dangerously high levels. My heart raced far beyond the normal pulse rate of 70 as tachycardia pushed it to 140 so often that it became a chronic condition.

(Chapter 14) My private office was very large and through a huge bay window I had a spectacular view of the glistening golden dome of the State House. As I sat in a comfortable swivel chair with a leather seat I could spin between two desks.

(Chapter 18) The hour I spent in the dazzling Light of the Presence of God provided answers to every question I ever had about my life and what it was all about. Since that day at the age of 53 my life as an orphan has made sense to me.

"Tom's Memoirs Are Written Like Novels."
--Jordan Rich, *WBZ News Radio*, Boston

Call Me An Orphan:

My Life as a Misfit

~~~~~~~~

A Psychological Memoir

~~~~~~~~

Tom O'Connell

(Author of *Upward & Downward Mobility*)

tomoconnellbooks

Call Me An Orphan:
My Life as a Misfit~
A Psychological Memoir
by Tom O'Connell

Published in the United States by
Tom O'Connell Books (aka Sanctuary Unlimited)
www.tomoconnellbooks.com
irishtommy@comcast.net
P.O. Box 25, Dennisport, MA 02639

This is a work of nonfiction.

This book was printed in the United States of America.

To order additional copies of this book, contact your Bookseller and refer to Ingram Book Company or go to Amazon.com or Barnes & Noble bn.com or contact Tom O'Connell Books at tomoconnellbooks.com.

ISBN: 978-0-9827766-2-9

www.tomoconnellbooks.com

Call Me An Orphan: My Life As a Misfit
By Tom O'Connell

In a candid, informal style, writer Tom O'Connell traces his life as a "misfit" from his early days in the 1930s and 1940s as an orphan in a Catholic Charities group home upward to top leadership roles in Massachusetts.

In a psychological memoir, he recalls challenging careers as CEO, educator, freelance writer, columnist, host of public affairs show "It's Your Life" on Boston's Channel 25.

The author says, "My point in writing this book is to share with others how it feels to be an orphan, to describe my status as an orphan, and also to relate how being an orphan affected the way I functioned during this long life of mine."

The memoir delivers a roller coaster ride of achievements as he moves up from Granny's duplex next to the railroad tracks to the Governor's Highway Safety Committee, CEO of Massachusetts Safety Council, inclusion in *Who's Who in the East*, and selection in *Cape Cod Life's* 25th Anniversary Issue as "one of the top 100 influential people" on Cape Cod.

O'Connell also tells how he plummeted from the heights into the serious challenges of divorce, illness, bankruptcy.

"Tom's memoirs are written like novels."
--Jordan Rich, *WBZ News Radio* 1030, Boston.

($15)

~~~~~~~~

"All sorrows can be borne if you put them into a story or tell a story about them." --Isak Dinesen, Author

~~~~~~~~

~~~~~~~~

Thanks

To the God of Love and Truth and to all who have helped me find my way through various life passages, challenging transitions, endurance tests, and intriguing mental labyrinths during this adventurous journey that we call life.

~~~~~~~~

Chapters

Epigraphs

"You will come to know the truth and the truth will set you free."

–Jesus The Christ

"Be still and know that I am God."

--Psalm 46

"The face of truth remains hidden behind a circle of gold. Unveil it, O God of light, that I who love the true may see!"

--Isa Upanishad

"To different minds, the same world is a hell, and a heaven."

--Ralph Waldo Emerson

"It is at once our loneliness and our dignity to have an incommunicable personality that is ours, ours alone and no one else's, and will be so forever."

--Thomas Merton

Call Me An Orphan:
My Life as a Misfit~
A Psychological Memoir
by Tom O'Connell

Chapter 1
Introduction

Call me an orphan. I'm okay with that word now. But it took me a long time to accept that description of where I fit into the demographics of life. Now I'm a senior citizen and I didn't start thinking of myself as an orphan until recently.

For most of my life I was an orphan but I didn't know that. Almost nobody ever called me an orphan. However, based on what I know now, I can say that I am an orphan and have been an orphan since my earliest months on this planet.

The Fourth Edition of the American Heritage College Dictionary helped me to confirm my reluctance to call myself an orphan. Definition 1a says an orphan is "A child whose parents are dead." That's exactly why I used to believe I did not qualify as an orphan. My parents were alive.

Finally, not very long ago, I took a close look at the 1b part of the definition that goes on to say, "A child who has been deprived of parental care and has not been adopted." Those words amazed me. They described me exactly.

Another part of the dictionary definition says, "One that lacks support, supervision, or care." And another part says, "Lacking support or supervision; abandoned." I can relate to those descriptions too. Especially the word "abandoned." Abandonment, of one kind or another, has haunted me over and over again during my journey through life.

In my early years, my basic identity hinged upon the fact that I was a Catholic Charities kid being raised in a home where five other boys from shattered homes lived. Like the other boys at Mrs. White's house, I had been thoroughly abandoned. In my case, my father did the abandoning.

We boys supported by Catholic Charities were not adorned with the designation of "orphan." That would have been an upgrade. Also, nobody around us called our house an orphanage. It was simply "Mrs. White's house."

When I arrived there at age five, these were the other five boys living there: John Desmond, Richard Roy, Bob Resker, Joe Rothwell and his brother David.

You might say that we did not have any specific designation except that we were Catholic Charities kids. That was all. And I don't think any of us wanted to pursue the subject. It was too sensitive to deal with.

During the nine years I spent with Mrs. White we boys never talked with each other about our status. Without any formal agreement, we just didn't discuss the past.

Looking back, I might simply say we had no status at all in society. We were in some kind of gap. And that provides nothing to talk about.

I know that's not a joyful perspective. Yet, until recently, the less anybody said about my family status in childhood the better. Why discuss it?

Based on the question I just asked, you might use a psychological term and conclude that I am afflicted with "Avoidant Personality Disorder." I would not disagree.

But the truth has a way of emerging even when we try to avoid it. For example, some person interested in my past might say to another friend, "Tom was raised in an orphanage."

I have a close friend who does that. He comes from a

small family with two children. So I guess he thinks my life at Mrs. White's house with five other abandoned boys was part of a group experience in an institutional setting that could be considered to be an orphanage.

Come to think of it, a newspaper reporter described Mrs. White's house as an orphanage when he reviewed my book *The O'Connell Boy: Educating "The Wolf Child"~An Irish-American Memoir (1932-1950).* But I could not relate to that description then. I relate to it better now.

At that time I wondered how Mrs. White's place with just six boys could be called an orphanage. I used to think an orphanage had to be housed in a large building like an Army barracks and contain lots of orphans. I still pretty much see orphanages that way.

My ongoing strategy about people's views on the life I lived when I was young was just to let people's comments pass. I became an expert at letting their remarks go in one ear and out the other, as folks used to say.

I have already pointed out that I did not have two dead parents. In my early years I had no idea where my mother was but I knew I had a mother somewhere. And I would see my father sometimes so I knew he was alive. That being the case, how could I be an orphan?

As I grew older I probably could have tried to explain my situation to anybody who asked questions, but in any group situation I was "the quiet one." I carefully avoided making comments about my past. Why would I tell people that my mother was incurably insane and lived in an insane asylum?

Actually, I avoided making comments about many things, especially the ones that mattered to me. I was painfully shy, a fundamental introvert who had a lot going on in my own head. Wasn't that enough to deal with?

Both in childhood and as an adult I hated the idea of explaining anything to anybody about my thoughts or how I had spent nine years from age 5 to 14 in a Catholic Charities home run by a ferocious Irish widow.

In recent years, sometimes I might wisecrack about my origin and say, "I came here from another galaxy and arrived here by spontaneous combustion." When I said something like that, I felt there might have been some truth in it.

Several years ago, as I read another review about one of my books, I noticed that the home where I was raised was again called an orphanage. So this time I shrugged and said to myself, "The reviewer just doesn't understand."

I think one of the basic feelings of my whole life has been the feeling I was often misunderstood. Even if some people wanted to understand the life I had lived, how could they?

Hey, I couldn't understand my own life never mind explain it. So why even bother explaining a confusing past to people who obviously will misunderstand?

Naturally, I tended to be a very quiet young man. It was probably in my nature to be quiet anyhow, but the childhood trauma provided an additional explanation for my silence. Being quiet was a good defense.

I am aware that I'm very much like those military veterans who had an overdose of combat during a war and avoided discussing it when they returned to civilian life.

Looking back, I think the group of us boys at Mrs. White's house could have been accurately described as "displaced persons suffering from PTSD." But decades ago the "displaced persons" description was mainly used for folks who were in transit as DPs after a major war or a serious natural disaster.

Posttraumatic stress disorder was an unfamiliar term that was not understood very well and still is not fully grasped. Actually, I think the understanding of PTSD is superficial.

I've always related to DPs and their disasters. I relate to the shocking experiences they have had. And I suppose an objective person looking at my own life might consider it to be a puzzling sequence of periodic unnatural disasters.

The six of us kids at Mrs. White's place came from what some people used to think of as "broken homes." But we were not called "broken home kids" or "misfits."

Today if somebody called me a misfit I would just nod my head and agree. I used to think "misfit" was an insulting word. Not now.

Mrs. White was listed as our "guardian" on our report cards from school, and when she described us orally she simply called us "Mrs. White's boys." I can remember her doing that while giving us pep talks. "Mrs. White's boys are not going to bring shame on this house." She certainly didn't say "My wards" or "My orphans."

She acquired us from the Catholic Charitable Bureau of the Archdiocese of Boston and she always took six boys. Not five. Not seven. Always six boys. No girls.

With Catholic Charities in those days it was usually a temporary arrangement. There were no legal adoptions at Mrs. White's house. If conditions changed in the family of origin and the boy's relatives could take responsibility again, a boy could depart shortly without complications.

Just to be sure there is no confusion on how I dealt with my own status during the nine years when I was living at 42 Mountain Avenue in Norwood, Massachusetts from 1937 at age 5 to 1946 at age 14, let me clarify.

If I was trying to describe myself to someone in Norwood who asked a personal question about my family, I would usually say, "I'm one of Mrs. White's boys." Or I might say, "I live with Mrs. White." For me, that was enough.

If that prompted more questions I would just clam up. That was part of my avoidant approach. I was a natural when it came to clamming up. It's also a common strategy in minority cultures because historically in those cultures the way a person answered a question could lead to big trouble.

Minority populations such as the Irish used to be were obfuscation specialists. They were experts at conscious avoidance of hazardous comments.

In my case, I always avoided volunteering personal details about my life. I was an expert at beating around the bush. This was my way to protect myself. An orphan's way.

I think it's only natural that based on the unsolved mysteries of my family of origin, I hated people's questions. I especially hated admitting that I lived with Mrs. White.

After I found out about my mother's insanity I hated questions even more. If anyone asked about my parents I would think, "Why can't these people mind their own business and lay off the questions?"

Deep shame and intense embarrassment followed me through much of my life. How could I casually explain my mother's existence in an insane asylum? How could I say I had never seen her or her relatives since my early infancy?

How could I explain the way my father abandoned me repeatedly and then dumped me into a Catholic Charities home when I was five and left me there for nine years?

The very thought of any of these scenarios filled me with deep shame at every stage of my life. I never got used to my reality. I hid it. I sidetracked it. I dodged it. Reality might be a healthy place to visit but I had no intention of living there.

If the final stage of the grief process is acceptance, you might think I never completed the final stage. You might believe that grief might be my underlying emotional state during much of my life. Well, you would be correct.

If I had lost my parents in an auto accident there would be some grief but no shame. It would just be an unfortunate twist of fate. And I would accept that reality.

My mother's insanity and my father's habit of abandoning me were sources of deep shame and confusion with no resolution. So I had some specialized shame to deal with and embarrassment that stayed with me a long time.

When I eventually became a freelance writer in 1978 to escape being a work slave, it was also a protective strategy. Writers ask the questions, not those whom they interview.

Being a freelance writer was a good place for a shame-based eccentric social misfit. I was too traumatized to describe my own situation adequately and openly without inflicting a jarring dose of emotional pain on myself.

I could describe other people's traumatized lives well, but not my own. I tried to keep it buried. But it kept coming back to life. There were so many mental blocks to hurdle.

Essentially, as I look back now, my fundamental problem was that I hated being different. I know it would have been easier for me if I could have adjusted to being different. But for most of my life I was never satisfied with the cards that were dealt to me.

"Could we give the deck another shuffle and deal me a new hand, please?"

So I envied kids who were "real" orphans with dead parents or who had been adopted. I especially envied kids who had parents and lived with them. In my prayers I would complain about this to God, who would reply with silence.

Sometimes I would have nightmares about my insane mother in a State controlled "snake pit." Other times I would have fantastic dreams about my mother reappearing and joining my father and me to lead a happy life together.

In reality, I lived my life with no mother and an inconsistent father who disappeared for varying periods of time and then reappeared for a short time like a person in a dramatic performance on a theater stage.

That surrealistic version of my life, like a Fellini movie, was the actual life I lived from my earliest times. And the solitary silent star of the show was me, the orphan.

I wish to emphasize that except for the circumstances I have already cited, when I was young I was not called an orphan, nor did I ever hear anybody else call Mrs. White's Mountain Avenue home in Norwood an "orphanage." Nor did I hear somebody call it a "group home" or a "foster home." It was just "Mrs. White's house." That's how it was.

After leaving Mrs. White's, when pressured to say where I had come from I used to say I had been raised in a foster home. But I knew that was not accurate. We were in the temporary care of Mrs. White. That's all there was to it.

Later I would sometimes say I was raised by my grandmother and skip any mention of my nine years at Mrs. White's house. In recent years I've been more open about my past and I'm likely to describe Mrs. White's as "a group home" or just say I was raised by Catholic Charities.

I may be belaboring this subject to get this book started, but I want you to know that right from the beginning of my life I had a strong aversion to admitting I had been a kid from Catholic Charities. And I didn't care much for being described as "one of Mrs. White's boys." Of all things, I was certainly not going to call myself a "foster kid" or "orphan."

Well, that's the way I began my nonconforming life. I was with Mrs. White from age 5 to 14. Nine years. Psychologically, those are important formative years. However, despite the events of my formative years, I'm sure that much of my personality originated in my DNA.

As I have watched my children, grandchildren, and even great grandchildren enter the world it has been obvious to me that some of them arrived on the planet with my DNA and possessed personalities and nervous systems similar to mine.

To me it's clear that my character was also affected by my chaotic first five years that I hardly remember, the nine years with Mrs. White that I remember with great accuracy, and the years after age 14 that I recall exceptionally well.

My excellent recall may be due to sensitivity, my life as a writer, a lecturer's talent for reflection on days gone by, the years I spent as an investigator for two different insurance carriers, and my extensive psychological education.

Just as those who have fought in active combat can be called veterans, I am a veteran of the outrageous harmful situations I experienced. Every life has its ups and downs, right? But some lives involve more extremes than others. You can be the judge of how extreme my life has been. I am simply telling my story.

This book is not an instructional manual but it is my hope that reading my memoir may trigger greater understanding of situations resembling mine. My basic point in writing this book is to share with others how I feel about being an orphan, to describe my status as an orphan, and to give some clues about how being an orphan affected the ways I functioned during this long life of mine.

For another perspective on my early years, you may enjoy *The O'Connell Boy: Educating "The Wolf Child"*. That book takes a close look at the years I spent from birth in 1932 until my first day at Boston College in 1950.

In my recent work memoir, *Upward & Downward Mobility,* my emphasis was on the details of my lengthy work life. Even though I am commenting on some work situations in this book, you will get a more thorough description of the energy I put into my careers if you obtain a copy of *Upward & Downward Mobility*.

In the current memoir I am taking a closer look at the psychological factors in the orphaned life I have lived.

Chapter 2
My First Five Years

I was born under the astrological sign of Aquarius on February 11, 1932 at about 5 pm in Dedham, Massachusetts, a Boston suburb proud of being "a colonial town rich in tradition." My difficult birth took place in a rented house on Curve Street in the blighted area called East Dedham.

The time of my arrival on this planet was in the depths of the Great Depression. Actually, I call it the First Great Depression since I am convinced that as I write this memoir in 2014 we are now living in the Second Great Depression. I say this because I have not seen so many empty businesses on formerly busy streets since I was a child in the late 1930s.

However, the politicians and the media propaganda machines have been describing this time as a "recovery" during several recent years of countless failed businesses, massive unemployment and underemployment, shrinking opportunities, and intentionally misinterpreted statistics. But that's another story you may gain some insight about if you read my book *Power, Politics & Propaganda.*

Most of the information about my early years is what my father Thomas Frederick O'Connell told me in brief bursts of alcohol induced truth when I was quite a bit older. I believe the most important fact is that when I was born it was an extremely difficult childbirth experience for me and my mother and father.

As background information, I need to tell you that my father was a candid conversationalist when he made up his mind to be straightforward. His directness could be stunning.

At any rate, he told me that after years of bliss with my mother "everything went downhill" when I was born. The major problem that my arrival on the planet triggered, he said, was the postpartum depression that disabled my mother Margaret Miriam Henderson O'Connell.

In other words, the very birth that brought me into the world also led to the breakup of my parents' happy married life, the loss of my mother to a variety of incurable mental health conditions, and a lengthy string of abandonments due to my father's decisions about my life.

To sum it up in a few words, my mother lost her mind shortly after my birth. Then she spent the rest of her life in Commonwealth of Massachusetts insane asylums in Boston.

I have no memory of her nor did I get to know her family. As far as I know, her relatives never visited me in any location where I lived.

Except for a very short time after my birth I never knew my mother. To connect with the unreality of my mother's existence, I have nothing but a few photos of her in an old album and a few more photos given to me by members of her family of origin at her wake after her death when I was middle aged.

Apparently, from my earliest days I was in the care of a succession of folks other than my mother. In my early thirties when I ran for a seat on Dedham's School Committee, a voter said, "You don't know me but when you were an infant you lived in my house for a while."

That lady's house was one of a number of temporary care situations where I was placed because of my father's inability to provide for my care himself.

As I learned about my early years in fits and starts I felt more and more like an emaciated Charles Dickens character. According to my father, I lived with relatives and strangers during the early years. He also said I lived in good Boston neighborhoods and the slums. I'm lucky I survived it all.

I survived my chaotic early years in various homes of strangers and for nine years at ferocious Mrs. White's house under the protection of Catholic Charities. Then I survived my undernourished adolescence and early adulthood as a self-directing free spirit under Granny O'Connell's roof.

However, I did not know until my adult years that during the time I was in Dedham and afterward there was a woman observing my development. She was reporting to my mother's family in Winthrop the information she received about me as I grew, some of it including newspaper stories about my election to the Dedham School Committee and appointment to the high profile Boston area occupations where I eventually held leadership positions.

For more insight into my connection to the world of work, please get a copy of *Upward & Downward Mobility: A Work Memoir~A Writer's Zigzag Journey*. I think you will enjoy it.

Later, my mother's family had the benefit of information about me that came to them from the mass media when I became well known in Massachusetts and a featured guest on leading TV and Radio discussion shows.

Now let's go back to the earliest part of my life. During my first year when I was about six months old I have no idea where I was living. But later my father said I experienced a collapsed lung and lost half my body weight before they got me to Children's Hospital in Boston. He said the hospital saved my life by "baking" my lung and other therapies.

By the time I was a year old my little brother Jackie, my only sibling, was born and our impaired mother was unable to be with either of us. So we were placed in separate temporary care situations.

My brother became very ill at the home where he was staying. Then he contracted a case of pneumonia, which was often a fatal disease in the 1930s.

My father told me that on my second birthday my year-old brother died in my father's car on the way to Children's Hospital in Boston. I still have a vague memory of seeing

Jackie in his casket in my grandmother's parlor. Wakes and funerals were usually in private homes in those days.

When I lost my brother I became "an only child." Also, that was my first experience of death involving somebody closely related to me.

Most of the losses I experienced during my life did not involve death, and in some ways I think they were worse. The person I cared about would suddenly be gone from my life with no explanation and I would be repeatedly left with a deep feeling of abandonment.

I have come to look at abandonment as a traumatic wound that never fully heals. It's the kind of wound that can easily drive a suffering person into various addictions and other escape mechanisms. I can attest to that. That is what I did.

Actually, I have learned from experience that each new abandonment intensifies the painful impact of the earlier wounds and keeps escalating. Once I made the mistake of telling a friend that I had already experienced everything that ever frightened me and that this provided an emotional shield against new wounds. I was so wrong about that conjecture.

Within days I experienced a new loss that practically floored me. So I came to realize that the wounds of betrayal and abandonment never heal completely. They remain deep inside, ready to surface when a new wound occurs.

Actually, I was bounced around in my early years like a lost piece of baggage with a missing destination label in an airport terminal. And the effects of such a start in life are beyond analysis. But I will provide some food for thought.

You might say that when I arrived on this planet at birth I rapidly became a very lonely visitor to this spinning world. Although words cannot adequately describe it, my viewpoint is that nobody knows the loneliness that lies in the heart of an orphan. Another orphan may know, but that's about it.

When I grew into adulthood I told myself that the

horrendous times were over and done with. But my wishful thinking was erroneous. Way off the mark. My memory stores all events and never fully forgets anything.

At any rate, my father told me that as my mother's condition worsened he arranged for her to return to her own family in Boston. He moved into my grandmother's side of her ancient duplex next to the East Dedham railroad station where he was destined to stay for many years. One of my uncles and his family lived on the other side of the duplex.

Apparently, I was an overly sensitive personality from the start. My father said I cried all the time and was very irritable. He also said my brother Jackie was good natured and always smiled. Yet I survived whereas Jackie died.

After my brother's death I continued to live in temporary care situations. And I had a screaming and crying fit each time I was relocated. I was not accepting what life was delivering to me. So I let the world know it.

"Shuffle the deck and deal me another hand of cards."

I believe that in 1934 or 1935, when I was a few years old, my mother was declared incurably insane. Then she was committed to the Commonwealth of Massachusetts insane asylum known as Boston State Hospital.

My father said that the last time we visited her we met her in the lobby of the asylum. According to him, when he handed me to my mother, she grabbed my little body and threw me away from her. My father said I landed in a potted plant that may have saved me from serious injury or death.

According to my father, he and I never saw my mother again after that episode. I continued to live with strangers until 1936 at age four when I joined my father in my grandmother's duplex at 22 Walnut Place in East Dedham.

For me, that was a very special place. Throughout my early life Granny's house was the only place in which I felt safe and at peace for any length of time.

I had lots of freedom there. Perhaps too much. In later years I was told that due to failing health my grandmother had not been able to keep up with me. So that's where Catholic Charities entered the picture.

Why was I so hard to keep up with? I would wander out of the house and explore the neighborhood. I would hide until I was found. I could be a very energetic little pest who had an excessive desire for freedom of movement.

In fact, an aunt told me many years later that when I was a few years old if somebody asked my name I would say, "Tommy O'Connell, DP." When they asked what DP meant I would say, "Damn pest." I must have heard someone say it.

So I was no easy kid to care for. Apparently, I had a mind of my own right from the outset and that quality has remained with me for a lifetime, with mixed results.

From my perspective, the most negative events at Granny's house were when my father would leave the house. He did this early in the morning to go to work at Dedham Post Office and he went out nearly every night. The moment I heard his car leave I had one of my extended crying binges.

There it was again, the crying that stemmed from the separation anxiety and attachment hunger that haunted me. I cried myself to sleep every night. With my abandonment syndrome, crying myself to sleep was standard behavior.

I do not believe that my grandmother ever came upstairs to the bedroom to pacify me. She was aging and uninvolved. Her own parenting years had ended decades earlier.

As I look back at the situation, I see that after losing my mother and being placed in the homes of strangers, my life became a succession of new forms of abandonment. This fixed the pain of being abandoned deeply in my psyche.

As I recall my early years I see that I lived in a stream of abandonments and never adjusted to it. Obviously, I was emotionally impaired in a way very similar to veterans of wars who had been deployed many times to combat zones.

Add to their number the veterans who had experienced being prisoners of war. I still shudder a little when driving and I see an Ex POW or MIA registration plate or bumper sticker. A dart jabs my psyche. Emotionally, I have spent long periods of time that resembled being a prisoner of war.

I have even coined a phrase to describe my impairment: "Exquisite Sensitivity." My "E.S." is a coin with two sides. The ups of life are often enjoyable yet they are accompanied by the awareness that they are going to be very short lived. The downs are excruciatingly painful. Finding a middle ground requires much internal effort and spiritual discipline.

The posttraumatic stress symptoms I was destined to carry with me are easily triggered. In my early years little was known about PTSD. Now we know that any traumatic loss or series of losses can trigger it.

The nature of the loss is usually something horrendous or "unthinkable." Even observing somebody else's loss can open the psychological wounds and result in a panic attack.

In Mrs. White's house where six boys were constantly getting into various kinds of trouble we all spent lots of time watching the other boys get punished, one at a time. Therefore, our PTSD triggers were constant.

For many years after departing from Mrs. White's house at age 14 I had what is described as a "startle response." If I were near another person and he or she suddenly raised a hand to deal with an itch or a stray hair I would instantly throw my arms upward and use my hands to protect my face from violence. Mrs. White had a violent nature and her perfectly maintained house was a violent place.

Over the years, in adult life I attended seminars, lectures and conferences about PTSD. I interviewed experts and I wrote about it when I was a national correspondent for *The U.S. Journal of Drug & Alcohol Dependence*. I also wrote about it when I was editor of Beech Hill Hospital's widely distributed newsletter about addiction treatment.

Beech Hill Hospital at Dublin, New Hampshire, was one of the leading addiction treatment centers in New England. For several years this fine healthcare facility was my largest consulting client. So I learned a lot about addiction from Beech Hill and did extensive writing for them about PTSD and other aspects of the addictive process.

PTSD is a chronic condition and is often a factor in the addictions that victims may turn to as they attempt to blot out the pain of the unmentionable wounding they have received. The wounds may be physical, mental, emotional, social or spiritual. Or a combination of these factors.

Without fear of contradiction, I can state that PTSD pain may be deeply buried but never fully erased. It can lead to a wide variety of psychological impairments.

One symptom that I am personally familiar with is the disabling panic attack. It can happen with no obvious trigger, without any warning. In its aftermath a person may be left feeling painfully vulnerable for an extended period of time.

Under the heading of "Anxiety Disorders" in the DSM-IV manual of Diagnostic Criteria produced by the American Psychiatric Association, you will find a very clear description of "Panic Attack."

On page 199 it is described as a "period of intense fear or discomfort." It provides a list of symptoms familiar to people who have a psyche like mine.

Here are some of the distressing panic attack symptoms I have had to deal with periodically throughout my life: palpitations, pounding heart, accelerated heart rate, trembling, shaking, shortness of breath, chest pain or discomfort, abdominal distress, feeling dizzy, unsteady, lightheaded, feelings of unreality, fear of losing control, fear of dying, tingling sensations, chills, hot flushes.

The desire to escape the repeatedly intrusive memories and effects of the trauma can lead to terrifying mood swings including severe anxiety and deep depression. PTSD is very hazardous to a person's health and should not be trivialized.

A common coping method when one has PTSD is to lose oneself in addictions. I know this from my own experience and the experience of others who have shared a similar fate.

Naturally, PTSD is often a factor in a wide variety of mental health and nervous system disorders. It needs much more attention individually and throughout society. It has been a very important factor in my own personal development and will continue to be.

During May 1976, in a series of examinations at Boston's world renowned Lahey Clinic when I was 44 years old, my attending physician and a clinical psychiatrist were trying to gain a deeper understanding of my possibly "psychosomatic" physical disturbances and my mental tendency toward anxiety and depression.

So I was asked to perform the intensive Minnesota Multiphasic Personality Inventory (MMPI). The MMPI is a frequently used personality test in the field of mental health.

The following gives you some of the psychological highlights from my MMPI results and the psychiatric evaluation that followed a few weeks later:

- Highly rebellious and nonconformist
- Touchy, sensitive
- Artistic, bohemian temperament
- Confused feelings, moody
- Moderately depressed, worrying
- Restless or agitated

The words "posttraumatic stress disorder" were not used when the situation was explained to me. Nor were the initials PTSD included then. But a person with my test results could now be viewed as a candidate for the PTSD diagnosis.

When I first read my medical file and found the results, I thought they had exaggerated. But as I review my life in this psychological memoir I don't find a problem with the report.

Looking back on my life in this memoir, it is very clear to me that I have had periodic bouts with painful trauma throughout my life.

Obviously, there were deep wounds from my perilous early years in temporary care situations. There were emotionally and physically painful years spent in the Catholic Charities home where violence was quite common.

There was the distress of periodic poverty. Also, there was the distressing tension of my Army years. Often there was indescribable stress in my high profile occupations.

In addition, there was the stress of family life in a marriage that lasted nearly thirty years. Eventually, there was separation and finally a challenging divorce after that marriage ended. Also, there were periodic bouts of life-threatening illness such as "garden variety" prostate cancer.

The late 1960s and the 1970s were a horrendous time in my occupational and emotional life. Actually, I have had major challenges to face during every period of my life, but those years were so trying I wonder how I survived them without going mad or dying from nervous exhaustion.

In total, I can say I have been lucky to have survived a wide variety of "unthinkable" experiences.

Note that when I just wrote the word "survived," I did not say I was "cured." But I could "function" and "adapt" to life to a surprising degree. Thank God for that.

God bless all of us who have experienced unthinkable trauma. To deal with our trauma and the ensuing PTSD that leaves lasting effects on our battered spirits, we need God's grace, patience, and the compassion of others.

Chapter 3
Mrs. White's House

The year 1937 opened one of the challenging periods in my early life. When I was 5-1/2 years old, just before entering the first grade of elementary school, I was taken without warning from my grandmother's house in the Boston suburb of Dedham. I was transported from East Dedham in my father's shiny new Plymouth to Mrs. White's house at 42 Mountain Avenue in Norwood, several miles away.

A fairly comprehensive account of my years with Mrs. White and later with Granny O'Connell can be found in my memoir *The O'Connell Boy: Educating "The Wolf Child"~~an Irish-American Memoir* (1932-1950).

My father accompanied me into Mrs. Margaret Monahan White's house with a very limited assortment of my worldly goods. I didn't have to take much with me to launch my new way of life. I could travel light. Mrs. White, the Irish widow serving as "guardian" for me and five other Catholic Charities boys in her care, would deal with my needs.

The new way of life that was inflicted on me was destined to last until 1946 when I would be 14 years old. But I was never informed about how long I would be expected to stay with Mrs. White. In those days children were not considered to be entitled to information about their lives. So my stay with Mrs. White was an indefinite sentence. Therefore, I can relate to the way some prisoners in jails would feel.

To express my total frustration with my state of abandonment at Mrs. White's place I started screaming and crying furiously. I began this behavior the moment we entered the.house. And I did not stop crying for several days.

The other five boys at the house said I set a record that broke all previous crying records. I cried day and night except for the times I fell into total exhaustion and slept.

I think I believed there was a chance of being retrieved by my father if I kept crying. This was the same misguided belief that had accompanied me throughout my early years of abandonment when I was repeatedly shipped from one living space to another, mostly with strangers and maybe once in a while with a relative.

I simply kept crying, based on the underlying belief that somehow my crying would get me released from the place I wanted to escape from and set me free in a place where I wanted to be. But my crying never achieved my goals. It only exhausted me and everyone else within earshot.

Naturally, I had to stop crying sooner or later. When I stopped it was not because I had suddenly accepted my situation. I could never simply accept the mysterious loss of my mother which had not been explained to me because her insanity was a family secret shrouded in stigma.

Nor could I accept the fact of being repeatedly abandoned by my father. How could I accept that reality in my five-year-old mind? How could I conceive of a father discarding his child? How could I "adjust" to such a fate?

I am speaking for myself, not other orphans, but for me there was never a healthy long term adjustment to my orphaned fate. At times I denied its impact on me. At other times I seldom thought about it. But its power has hovered in my psyche throughout my life. Separation anxiety and attachment hunger have followed me as persistent shadows.

In my life the final step of acceptance in the grief process was unattainable. It seems that memories of abandonments have always been near the surface of my conscious existence. Reminders were constant. And they still are. Especially on holidays and other special days.

Mother's Day has always been an emotional day of horror for me, but outwardly I have concealed that reality. It's my very private personal horror. I have shared it with a few others in healthy ways but I need to keep a lid on it.

Today, May 11, 2014, happens to be Mother's Day. It's sunny and warm here on Cape Cod. A beautiful day. At age 82 I am fortunate to be here on the planet to enjoy such beauty. And that's what I have been doing. But on this beautiful Mother's Day my orphan mind is still somewhat in the grip of horror about my mother's loss and her insanity.

One might think that this horror would have disappeared long ago. But the deep memory never forgets anything. And the constant repetition of Mother's Day messages in the mass media brings the wound to the surface of the nervous system. It's a loss that cannot be minimized or analyzed. It's chronic.

Father's Day for me is not much better. Holidays such as Thanksgiving and Christmas have always had a similar effect. They have always been reminders of the various abandonments I have experienced.

There has really been no end of such reminders. Living each day in Mrs. White's house full of discarded boys was a daily reminder for nine years that I was different from boys who were raised with their family of origin.

We boys were misfits. Nobody called us misfits but in my adult life I eventually realized that was the best word to describe my situation. When have I not felt like a misfit?

Mrs. White's house of misfits in Norwood was a violent place. She was not a gentle woman. She was a fierce disciplinarian. She was very strong and built like a Japanese wrestler. She could be easily provoked into smashing us so hard that she would knock us off a kitchen chair and send us skidding across the perfectly waxed linoleum floor so fast that we did not come to a stop until we hit the opposite wall.

Was this abuse? Of course, but in those days of popular physical punishment it was not considered abuse. It was the way most boys were raised. We were treated like uncivilized creatures who had to be severely punished or "corrected" for not conforming to rules of the house or school or any other institution of allegedly civilized society.

Where do you think "correctional" institutions and "reform" schools got their names? The American Heritage Dictionary tells us that "Correct" means "conforming to standards." "Reform" means "to change for the better." Mrs. White was an expert at correcting and reforming.

At Mrs. White's when someone was being punished the rest of us were ordered to line up and watch her inflict the pain that was the consequence for the crime of breaking her laws. "I'll put the fear of the Lord into ye!" she would shout at the victim. Then she would look at us and add "I'll put the fear of the Lord into the lot of ye."

Watching another person being severely punished and reacting to extreme pain and suffering leaves its own psychological wounds. These wounds, as I have already noted, create scars that never completely heal. Those scars are closely connected to the PTSD syndrome.

As God's self-appointed representative on the planet, Mrs. White did not believe in half measures. In her eyes, each punishment had to fit each crime. A crime like swearing involved the mouth, so she would pour a mixture of brown Kirkman's laundry soap and warm water down our throats until our eyes watered and our throats gagged. We were not likely to forget that dramatic corrective treatment.

The most common punishment in Mrs. White's house was "the switch." We had to go outdoors to the nearby woods or the field across the street and get a small branch from a large bush. Then we had to strip all leaves from it and bring it back to Mrs. White. We had created a wooden whip.

The switches she liked best were about as thick as a person's little finger. If you didn't provide that she would send you out for other switches until you brought her what she needed for the punishment. And she was very fussy.

The switch was very effective with her strength behind it. I can still hear it as it came whooshing through the air before striking. And when it whipped against my rear end or the bare calves of my legs the intense pain was extreme.

Mrs. White never did anything lightly and as she whipped us it seemed that each switching was worse than the previous one. As a result, the very thought of getting the switch was enough to instill panic while one waited for the inevitable torture to be inflicted on our tender youthful skin.

The after effects of switching remained for days after the event. And that made the switching all the more effective. Although the switch was the most effective and most common method of punishing us, she had a whole variety of punishments that would fit the various crimes. Being closed up in a dark closet. Confinement to the cellar or the attic. And a whole array of burdensome tasks.

But the worst punishment of all was having her shove your head into the toilet in the cellar. She would hold your head down while she activated the overhead flush box. This involved much choking, gasping and other memorable symptoms. You were not likely to forget this punishment.

Life in that house of physical and emotional pain produced in me the acceleration of an early conscious life full of fantasies about being elsewhere, anywhere, away from the place where I lived. It was a life of unrealized desires, unfulfilled wishes, and fantastic fantasies.

In my overactive mind I was a child with an extremely lively imagination that I seldom shared with anybody else. I was the boy Mrs. White called "the quiet one." But my mind was never quiet. It was endlessly active. Usually overactive.

Mrs. White also used the word "refined" about me. How could I be refined if I was only five years old? I think it is because some people, especially the quieter ones, are born with self-contained tendencies that come with the DNA, family inheritance, or even the unseen world of the spirit which is such a mystery and produces "old souls."

I led a life with numerous compartments. I was one of Mrs. White's boys at her perfect house in Norwood, a Catholic Charities kid, an outstanding student, a compulsive reader, a quiet observer of others, and at the same time a member of the very dysfunctional and extremely eccentric O'Connell family of East Dedham.

Among other things, I was a student at Cornelius M. Callahan Elementary School in Norwood. I was a Roman Catholic Christian. I was an active member of St. Catherine of Siena Parish in the town of Norwood and less active at St. Mary's in Dedham after moving to East Dedham.

There certainly was no lack of educational motivation in my life. Before I went to school, in times when public schools did not have kindergartens, I was educating myself.

Before age 5, when I lived with Granny O'Connell, I asked other boys on Walnut Place to teach me the alphabet so I could read. I was fascinated with words and was reading skillfully by the time I entered the first grade.

In later tests of reading skill in elementary school I was always ranked at the very top of my class. Obviously, I had inner resources that provided self-esteem which was not supplied by other sources. I was satisfied with my mind but not with my body. Nor with my misfit existence.

I had a mix of high and low self-esteem that was very compartmentalized. I was proud of my excellent mind but I was embarrassed by my very thin physique and my overly prominent teeth and ears. And my misfit situation.

In the first six grades I received straight-A report cards and had the reputation of being "the smartest boy" in my class at the Callahan School. Also, I won all the spelling bees. So I considered myself superior mentally.

Yet I carried the stigma of being an outcast from my family of origin. And I was a Catholic Charities kid who had an insane mother. These realities haunted me but I could not discuss my truth with anybody else. I carried the burden of terrifying secrets. I felt like a spy in an enemy country.

My fascination with words blossomed in the fifth grade when I won a contest for the best essay about the war effort. We were in the middle of World War II and I wrote how our school raised funds to help purchase a jeep for the war effort.

The essay was published in the *Norwood Messenger*, a popular local weekly newspaper. That was the beginning of my desire to become a published writer some day.

At Norwood Junior High I became co-feature editor of *The Junior Narrator,* the school magazine. Later, in Dedham High School I was too lazy to get involved in the high school news publication but finally I became a writer on the staff of the graduating class of '49 yearbook named *Reflections*.

So, as a youth I was a writer in fits and starts but I never stopped being a reader. I was always reading books of my own choice. That was one of my precious freedoms in a world where my freedom was greatly restricted by the demands of living under Mrs. White's jurisdiction and being a member of her work crew with its many tasks.

My favorite reading was fiction, especially mysteries, whether it was the Hardy Boys or Charlie Chan or Sherlock Holmes. Once I came across an author like Jack London I would go along the public library shelf one book at a time until I had read everything the author wrote.

The people around me never quite understood my preference for reading instead of other worldly activity. But I did not really care about other people's opinions on what I enjoyed. From an early age, I felt it was none of their business. It was my business…period.

I have to give credit to Mrs. White for emphasizing that

we each had to live our own life and that it made no difference what the other kids were doing or thinking. This applied to neighborhood kids and kids at school or even the other kids in her house. "Think for yourself," she would repeat over and over to make the message indelible.

Of course, when the other boys in Mrs. White's house felt like playing baseball and I was engrossed in a book, then there was some emotional conflict. I hated conflict. So I would reluctantly participate in the sports and other boys' activities both inside the house and outdoors.

However, because I was skinny and lazy physically I didn't excel at sports. I could hit a baseball or whack a hockey puck but my mind was obsessed with my reading and I always wanted to get back to my book.

"You're gonna turn into a book," one of the other boys would say. I would just retort, "So what?"

Another thing I have always been grateful for about Mrs. White was her set of values about the world of the mind. Although most of the boys at her house did not come from families with wealth, she was always impressing us with the need to get a college education eventually no matter what the cost or how long it took.

She had put her son Tom through Boston College after her husband had died. So he became a role model for me. He was a fine young man who would pat me on the head as I walked by him. He called me "Tomaso" and provided some actual affection in a household where violent punishment was common and affection was rare.

To differentiate me from Mrs. White's son, the other boys in the house called him "Big Tom" and me "Little Tom" during the years he lived in the same house with us before graduating from Boston College. Then he went off to war and became a U.S. Marine officer in World War II.

I think he may have set the pace for the boys at Mrs.

White's when it came to higher education. Most of the boys who had lived with her went on to college.

This also meant that she had respect for my tendency to do a lot of reading. She was very pleased with my straight-A report cards and the way I won all the spelling bees. For her boys, any activity that meant we were doing well in school brought praise and encouragement.

For me, junior high was a different story. I slacked off because I no longer wished to be "the smartest boy." She knew I was slacking off with my Bs and a C once in a while. So she kept reminding me to do my best.

With Margaret Monahan White, doing one's best was extremely important. She applied this principle to everything she did and she expected us boys to do likewise. Her idea of "best" might have been hard on the people she lived with, but her values were excellent for the most part.

One of my values has always been my belief in the need for continuity in friendships. But this value was challenged when I was leaving the sixth grade. The two Rothwell brothers, Joe and Dave, left Mrs. White's at that time and went back to the Hyde Park section of Boston to live with their widowed father and about a dozen brothers and sisters.

The departure of the Rothwell brothers was extremely hard for me to take emotionally. This was a huge loss. I was very close to the two of them, especially Dave. We were best pals. And I could not picture functioning at Mrs. White's with no close friend in the house.

All I could think of was getting back to East Dedham and living with Granny so I would be nearer to the Rothwells. Dedham bordered on Hyde Park where they lived and it would be easy for us to see each other.

From East Dedham it would only be a quick bus ride. Or a ride on my Columbia bicycle. That would work fine. But not if I had to spend three more years in Norwood at the local junior high.

I felt that I was receiving another huge abandonment when my father stated that I could not return to Granny's house until I completed three more years at Mrs. White's. That would put me at age 14 and entering the sophomore year of Dedham High School.

To my father that meant I would then be pretty much able to take care of myself. His plan made sense to him but not to me. From my point of view, it was one more example of my father being my adversary instead of my mentor.

In a world where I basically distrusted people due to my traumatic experiences, my father was one person I tried to believe was worthy of my trust. Yet his track record for reliability with me tended to fall very short of the mark. Throughout my early life he delivered one disappointment after another to me with frustrating consistency.

The result? I plunged into deeper, darker loneliness although I was living in a very busy household. At any given time, there were usually about a dozen people at 42 Mountain Avenue. Mrs. White. Her son Tom. Jim Dervan, a neighbor who chose to live with us. Mr. Vincent the boarder. A couple of Irish immigrants she was sponsoring, such as Malachi and Ted Kelliher. And the six of us boys.

Now the Rothwells were gone and I was very angry about my situation. But what could I do? I was powerless to change it. So I felt totally abandoned, once again.

I believe as I entered that phase of my youth I dropped into a depression of sorts that affected my attitude toward just about everything, except my reading. It's a good thing I had my books to fall back on. They were my therapy.

The Norwood Library was one of my favorite places. It had a virtually endless supply of the kinds of books that I enjoyed. And I think that one of the very special moments of my young life was when I received my own library card. If I was in a low state of mind, I could always lift myself up by reading a good book.

Looking at myself objectively, I can see that I have always been a moody person. But I have usually kept my moods to myself. Who would be interested in them? They were my own business and that was that.

My customary attitude as I moved toward my early teen years was well summed up by the following quotations: "So what?" "Big deal." "Who cares?" "I couldn't care less."

But these were not phrases used within earshot of Mrs. White. In her house, negativity and sarcasm were as taboo as swearing and most questions.

She was not exaggerating when she said, "Children should be seen and not heard." She did not do opinion polls and survey the moods and feelings of the six boys in her care to learn our views. Our views meant nothing to her.

Mrs. White never asked for our opinions about anything that I can recall. But on special occasions she might give us a choice between two different items on the kitchen table.

Basically, we had to develop our own coping skills to make our lives more palatable. In addition to my tendency to lose myself in reading books, it was also good that another boy in my neighborhood was usually there to be my pal.

John Flaherty was that boy and we were pals throughout our three junior high school years. Across the street at 47 Mountain Avenue I spent more time hanging out with John in his room with the short wave radio than I did in the third floor finished room at Mrs. White's.

I shared that room with the two younger boys that had replaced the Rothwells. But I had nothing in common with the new arrivals except sharing the space.

With John as my pal I had an open door available to me at the Flaherty house where there was no discipline that I ever noticed. John had amazing freedom and both he and I could come and go as we pleased with no questions asked.

John was talented at assembling kits for radios, especially the short wave kind. He installed a huge antenna on his roof and we could listen to radio broadcasts from England and other places around the world. This was a kind of adventure in its own right because we could listen to foreign broadcasts about World War II.

As I reflect on that time in my life I can see that I was becoming more and more of an escapist. Escaping to John's house. Escaping into my books. Escaping from the perfect academic record I had achieved in elementary school. Escaping into mediocre academic performance. Trying to escape from the haunting consciousness of memories about my mother's insanity and her institutionalization.

Escaping, always escaping. That was my alternative to accepting my reality. The Irish are known for being dreamers, but in my case along with night dreams and day dreams I tended to have nightmares that were even more frightening than my life with Mrs. White.

I did more than my share of sleepwalking too. Luckily, I did not fall down the long winding flights of stairs leading to and from our third floor sleeping quarters.

As for Mrs. White's wishes, when I was a teen they seemed to be a kind of bondage even though I knew she was right about most of her ideas on life. She had very high standards. The standards of a perfectionist.

There were certain standards I maintained too. I might get Bs in junior high but rarely did I get a C. It was difficult for me to feign mediocrity. All the skills I had refined in elementary school were deeply imbedded. So it was not easy for me to pretend to be less intelligent than I was. Yet I did. I was sick and tired of being the smartest boy so I had downgraded myself from an A student to a B student.

Later on, when I graduated from Sunday School at St.

Catherine's I actually got a certificate for perfect attendance for the full nine years. So the perfectionism and the spiritual focus were still there despite my efforts to cover them up.

Although I used swear words more and more during junior high I would never say "fuck." To me, that word symbolized the worst language offense anybody could make. I mostly limited myself to "hell" and "damn" and "shit." My friend John had the opposite philosophy and thoroughly enjoyed his own frequent use of the word "fuck."

Even though I began to swear habitually, I never swore in Mrs. White's house. Although she expressed an abundance of anger I never heard her or anyone else in that house indulge in swearing. It was just not done and we knew it could not be tolerated. The consequences would be painful.

As the years in Norwood passed, my spiritual life grew along with my physical body and my intellectual mind. I followed most of the rules of the Catholic faith that I learned during my years as one of Mrs. White's boys.

The spiritual training was ongoing. Weekly confession and Communion. Mass every Sunday, on Holy Days of Obligation, and every day during Lent. Prayers before bedtime and on waking in the morning. Spiritual reading. Saying the Rosary together as a family group.

For the Rosary we would take the kitchen chairs, turn them around with the backs facing the table, kneel on the seat of the chair, and fold our hands on top of the backrest. There was no way to escape Mrs. White's rituals. Attendance was compulsory. Excuses were not permitted.

The way of life in Mrs. White's house was unchanging. She provided a very consistent environment where the word "compromise" was not part of her vocabulary. Yet she was not fanatically rigid about all of her ideas. She could change.

For example, her attitude toward the older boys in her care changed dramatically the moment we went from knickers to long pants. This took place after the sixth grade as we moved into the seventh grade and junior high school.

We transitioned into being young men at that time. No longer were we punished physically except on rare occasions. She would deny us privileges instead, such as prohibiting us from hearing our favorite radio programs and attending movies.

When it came to the opposite sex, we were not instructed on how to behave with girls. We were only told to avoid them. For adults in those days, the less said to young people about sex the better. Open discussion of sex did not exist in most homes. This was especially true with Mrs. White.

I don't recall ever seeing a girl enter our house to associate with one of us boys. When her son Tom White was engaged to marry beautiful Georgia Newman, obviously she was in and out of the house frequently. But she was an exception to Mrs. White's anti-female rules and regulations.

Mrs. White was not hesitant about expressing her strong bias against girls. She often cautioned us about the trouble they could get us into. For example, they could sidetrack us when it came to achieving our educational goals.

Actually, if the word "sex" was used at Mrs. White's on rare occasions it had to be spelled out: "S-e-x." As a result, our sexual education was a very private experimental set of experiences. Inside the house we acted pure and wholesome. Outside down at the woods it was another story.

Also, we were exposed to outrageous self-appointed mentors who were addicted to sexual "bragging." These were the older boys at school, on the playground, or at the Norfolk Golf Course caddie shack. They considered it their duty to pass on their lurid sex stories to the younger boys.

Mrs.White's boys spent considerable time during our adolescent years at Norfolk Golf Course. It was an earthy training program. Thorough descriptions of life in Mrs.

White's house and at the caddie shack are provided in my book *The O'Connell Boy: Educating 'The Wolf Child.'*

As I look back and try to be objective about my nine years with Mrs. White at 42 Mountain Avenue in Norwood, I can see that she gave me an excellent foundation for developing the right attitudes about education and career success.

She also gave me some fine religious fundamentals but the element of fear was overdone. In addition, the fear factor was a major tool she used to discipline us and train us for life. Much of that fear had to be overcome by me in later years and offset by confidence and love. Since I had an undercurrent of anxiety within me since infancy, this was easier said than done. But I tried to be confident and loving.

In my case, the feeling of imprisonment during those nine years was always there too, hovering near the edge of my awareness. It was accompanied by a ferocious desire for individual freedom when the time finally came for me to be released from Mrs. White's care.

I was released at the beginning of summer in 1946. That was the start of a season of total freedom as a caddie at Saranac Inn in New York's Adirondack Mountains.

"Free at last! Free at last!"

That season in my adolescent life has been graphically described in my memoir *The O'Connell Boy: Educating 'The Wolf Child.'*

My summer at Saranac Inn after leaving Mrs. White's house was a major transition in my early life. Crossing that bridge at age 14 was a fascinating adventure for me. It came at an ideal time. And it holds a special place in my memory.

Chapter 4
Freedom at Age 14

I don't think it's an exaggeration to say that Personal Freedom has been a key value in my life. Love has also been an important value, especially since I experienced such a serious Love deficit in my early years.

Love has confused me more than Freedom. The ideal of loving and being loved has been both a thrilling adventure for me sometimes and also an ongoing challenge. Or better still, it has been a continuing education. Eventually, I taught a course about it based on my book *Improving Intimacy.*

I need to admit that Love and Freedom have been mutually exclusive at times. The two values could stir up internal conflict within me and external conflict with others. Since I found conflict very annoying, I preferred a peaceful atmosphere with minimum conflict. So I avoided conflict.

Freedom was on my mind when I was released from Mrs. White's house in Norwood in 1946 at age 14. The ideal of individual liberty has not left me since then. Freedom is more than a privilege or a right; it is my individual mandate.

Mrs. White ran a tight ship, as they used to say. She was dynamic and fanatic about her own power. In today's world she might be described as a control freak. When a control freak is in charge of an enterprise, anxiety becomes the prevalent state of mind of all subordinates.

As a female version of Captain Ahab, every detail of the ship Mrs. White controlled at 42 Mountain Avenue in Norwood was subject to her scrutiny. Also, being a complex personality, she was her own fiercely independent white whale Moby Dick as well as Captain of her own vessel.

I see the white whale symbolizing her perfectionism. As she met her responsibilities she was more scrupulous than

Herman Melville was with his descriptions of Ahab's pursuit of the white whale. But instead of intending to slaughter Moby Dick, she was out to perfect her whale and everything connected with it. Her harpoon was aimed at imperfections.

Actually, Mrs. White was the self-proclaimed instrument of God's will for my nine years with her, from 1937 until 1946. God's will was not to be challenged. Nor could one challenge the will of God's representative in the person of the Irish immigrant widow named Margaret Monahan White.

Upon my release from the perfectionist care of God's representative, I knew that after I left 42 Mountain Avenue in Norwood I was bound to meet other difficult authority figures. But I also knew in my spirit from that day forward I would truly answer to no less of a higher authority than God.

Catholic Charities released me to the care of my father and grandmother at age 14, but I knew Granny would be neither my care giver nor my authority figure. She was too old to deal with a teenager like myself. Her energy was certainly limited by age and infirmity.

As for Fred, obviously he was too caught up in his own life to let my life distract him. He had already proved this interpretation and had always been very skilled at keeping me from becoming a high priority. True to form, I knew he would continue to avoid being a meaningful presence in my life. And I could live with that.

So at age 14 I became truly free and knew that at Granny's I would basically be on my own. How would I handle my new freedom? Naturally, it would take me a while to adapt to it just as it had taken my grandfather Dan the barber time to meet the challenges of his own life.

At age 14 Dan O'Connell had run away from home, apprenticed himself to a barber, and eventually operated his own barbershop. Fending for himself, he never looked back.

Spending the summer of 1946 at the upscale Saranac Inn

caddie camp in upstate New York's Adirondack Mountains was the ideal way to make my transition from rigid authority to virtually unlimited individual freedom. Also, my first Social Security card was provided by Saranac Inn.

My grandfather had run away from home to achieve his freedom; I had simply been freed from captivity at Mrs. White's by my father. He had told me years before that his eventual goal was to locate me at Granny's house at an age when I would be able to take care of myself. The age was 14.

At the caddie camp the young men were pretty much on their own. There was no central authority figure to be feared. The camp was not organized by a control freak. It was organized very loosely and that suited me.

I don't recall anybody in our dormitory being in charge. We simply slept in bunks there. In an adjacent hall we ate our meals. And we were fed very well. We were not operating like members of a military organization. There was no discipline that I can recall.

A married couple was overseeing the operation but they were not authoritarians. They were in charge of the kitchen and every other aspect that related to the caddies who ranged in age from the early teens to the late teens.

The two overseers passed out your mail if you had any. If you got a cut or any other kind of wound they attended to it with first aid or arranged transportation to medical care. That was about it.

Caddying at the adjacent exclusively private golf course kept us busy daily. When the day was done after eating supper we were free to do as we pleased. We didn't have to sign out or in. The older caddies were accustomed to making their own decisions. For the younger boys, freedom was a new and liberating experience.

Freedom can be daunting for those unaccustomed to it. You might imagine that this level of freedom was intoxicating for a fourteen-year-old like me. And you would be absolutely right.

Fortunately for me, I had pals from my days at Mrs. White's, Dave and Joe Rothwell, for companionship. So there was no major adjustment about coping with the new environment or making brand new acquaintances. I was free to relax with my pals and free to be me.

Later John Flaherty, my pal on Mountain Avenue across the street from Mrs. White's, also joined us at the caddie camp. The four of us made the most of our freedom.

As caddies and employees of the elite enterprise known as Saranac Inn we had access to Saranac Lake for swimming and boating. We could also use the high quality stable where the Inn kept their finely groomed horses.

We swam, rode horses, paddled canoes and guide boats, and set up campfires in the woods near the lake. Naturally, we sang songs that would be banned by adults. "Roll me over in the clover, roll me over, lay me down and..."

For me, the horseback riding did not become a lifelong pursuit. One day I mounted a horse that was supposed to be a gentle mare but turned out to be a freedom loving stallion. He took me for the ride of his life and mine on paths through the forest that I had never traveled before.

Branches of trees whacked at me and I could not stop the adventurous stallion. He ran until his energy flagged and, lucky for me, I remained on his back as he calmly trotted to the stable. That was the last time I rode a stallion.

When we got bored with life at Saranac, which was like a recreational Fantasy Island in the mountain wilderness, my pals and I went out to the highway and stuck out our thumbs. Our hitchhiking adventures were numerous.

Not yet at driving age, we seldom had access to a car unless it was as a passenger in one of the older guys' vehicles. On one of these occasions there was a terrible auto accident. Luckily, I missed being part of it.

I was betting on the side in a game of blackjack that night when asked if I would like to go for the joyride toward the Canadian border. I opted out because I was busy gambling.

The boys who accepted the ride included some of my pals. I learned later that the car was traveling at very high speed in a remote area when it went out of control and dove end over end into a swampy area with many trees.

The car plunged through the swamp, bounced off trees, propelled boys out of the open doors, and finally came to rest. One of the boys landed under the car where the hot exhaust pipe pressed down on his back. But the spongy nature of the swamp helped keep him from serious injuries.

Those were the days before seat belts were standard equipment in cars, so all of the boys were injured to some degree. Most of them required hospital care which ended their summer in the Adirondack paradise. They returned to their homes much earlier than originally planned.

A short time later, those of us who were not in the accident gravitated toward our favorite thumbing destination, the world famous Lake Placid. On one occasion our ride dropped us off in the outskirts of town at a local gas station where a couple of us met a few girls our own age.

This led to some pleasant friendships. As I recall it, I was the only one who continued to see two of the girls during much of the summer. The details of that part of my story can be found in the pages of *The O'Connell Boy* memoir.

I was especially smitten with one of the young ladies but was terrified of getting very involved with her or any other girl. After all, I was just fourteen and about to go into the sophomore year of Dedham High School. I was as unsophisticated as a young man could get.

Also, Mrs. White's warnings about girls registered deeply in my mind. Although I was attracted by the beauty of one of the girls, I was less threatened emotionally by her friend. So her friend and I became good pals. We had enjoyable times together and did lots of good natured kidding back and forth.

I did much solitary hitchhiking from Saranac to Lake Placid that summer until things changed. Suddenly the caddying job was terminated. The boys at the caddie camp had the bright idea that we could increase our pay by going on strike. The vote to do this was unanimous. So we struck.

Without delay the management at Saranac Inn decided they would not cave in to a bunch of aggressive teens. They informed us that they had lined up a crew of other boys to replace us. We were formally terminated. So the outcome of our attempt at unionization resulted in unemployment.

It was early in August and it seemed too soon for me to go back to Dedham. So I began to hang out each day with the girls I had befriended at Lake Placid.

I spent the first night there sleeping in the hay near the cows in a barn across the street from the home of the girl who was my platonic friend. I was concerned that one of the cows might step on me while I was asleep. So I did not sleep much that night.

The next day the girl told her parents about my homeless plight and they generously agreed to let me stay in a spare bedroom for a few days. I ended up at her house for the next few weeks. Then it was time for my trek back to Dedham.

Before heading for Granny's house I dated the pretty girl who had stolen my heart. During my brief romance with her I had the confusing pleasure of my first real kiss. I was really smitten by that young lady and for a while we wrote love letters to each other. But eventually it became obvious that I was not going back to the Lake Placid area again. Because I had no idea how to end a romance, I simply avoided replying to some of her letters. And that ended the romance.

Early in September 1946, after I had said goodbye to my

first romance, it was time to head for Granny O'Connell's house in Massachusetts. I started out with a Trailways Bus from Lake Placid to Albany, New York. But the ticket took me only to Albany where I ran out of money.

From Albany the fourteen-year-old lone wolf orphan completed an all night hitchhiking trek through New York and Massachusetts. The destination was East Dedham and Granny's duplex next to the railroad tracks.

The details of this adventure can be found in my memoir *The O'Connell Boy*. I kept sticking out my thumb throughout the night and after several hectic rides and a vagrancy challenge with the Pittsfield, Massachusetts police I arrived at my grandmother's house.

Home sweet ramshackle home. Granny's house was literally next to the tracks and the East Dedham station where folks got the Boston train. In back of her soot speckled house was a fence we called "the railroad fence." Our side of the tracks was "the wrong side." The other side was Oakdale, a desirable location.

But I was glad to be on Walnut Place in imperfect East Dedham, where I had felt most comfortable prior to age five when I was exiled to Norwood. Also, throughout the nine years at Mrs. White's house I had stayed with Granny and my father in East Dedham on many school vacations. So I was not a stranger there.

Since I had spent most of my youth in Norwood I knew I was pretty much of an outsider in Dedham. But I did not have to explain that to anybody. If I were asked about where I lived I could simply say, "I'm from East Dedham."

On vacations with Granny I had gotten to know kids in the Walnut Place neighborhood. So nobody there asked me personal questions. They knew my father worked in the Post Office and I don't recall anybody asking about where I had spent most of my time during the previous nine years.

I soon got in the habit of never mentioning my time with Catholic Charities and Mrs. White. It was nobody's business but mine, right? I was used to keeping secrets, so it took no great effort to do that during my Dedham High years. It was my secret. And that was that.

Since my favorite books were mysteries, it was as if I were in the process of creating my own living mystery with my hidden identity of being a former Catholic Charities kid.

Because I was quiet by nature it was not hard to maintain the silent fiction of always having been a Dedham resident. Actually, my return to Granny's duplex was a real homecoming. A very private one. And a very special one.

At age fourteen, I was a Dedham boy now, to all outward appearances. Yet I had a secret prior existence in Norwood that very few people knew about. And I was not about to enlighten them.

So it was no wonder that I became a very private person. Not anti-social. Just very private. And that's exactly how one of my three daughters described me recently.

She was not exaggerating. I have been a very private person throughout my life even though I have engaged in many very public career activities.

The thought enters my mind at this moment that I had been trained by Mrs. White in much the same spirit that future military men are trained at West Point. Their training is so effective that it lasts for a lifetime and affects much of what they do in life. Mrs. White's training was thorough.

In my early years with Mrs. White I was called "the quiet one." At age 82 I am still the quiet one who tries to follow Mrs. White's counsel to "Mind Your Own Business." In an increasingly complicated and noisy world I appreciate my peace and quiet more than ever. And I try to focus my mind on my own business.

Chapter 5
Transition to East Dedham & Granny

Just as my shyness was carried with me from home to home in my early years and then probably intensified during my nine years with Mrs. White, it was with me as I started living full-time in East Dedham in 1946 at age fourteen.

There is a very old expression about the human character that dates back hundreds of years. In simple terms, it suggests with a wry twist, "Wherever you go there you are." Using very similar words, this wisdom is found in one of the most widely read books the world has ever known: *The Imitation of Christ* by Thomas a Kempis.

As I relocated to 22 Walnut Place in East Dedham I was entering a different phase of my life. But the orphan reality was always with me. Everything else in my life could change but the inner orphan would always be there inside me.

Looking back at my life I see many inconsistencies. Yet my orphan misfit reality has remained constant and I have always qualified as "the outsider" in one way or another.

So the underlying reality of my life is summed up in the following quote, "Wherever I have gone, there the orphan has been." Looking objectively at my life I can say that what others may call my inconsistency has only meant to me that I was living an interesting life.

A colleague at work once said, "You are consistently inconsistent, Tom." He considered this a criticism. But I did not see his remark as an insult. I believe all of us are distinct individuals and we are free to be inconsistent. If I happen to be more distinctive or inconsistent than many others, so be it.

I think the same applies to families. No two families are alike. And no two people are just alike. So why do we try to invent categories to explain ourselves to others? The categories we enjoy creating to describe others and ourselves seldom come close to the reality.

Just as we can't judge a book by its cover, I think we all carry around a hidden personality inside us that we share only partially with a chosen few others. In my case, being a fundamental introvert, the true internal personality was in hiding much of the time until recent years.

I believe that what has been happening to me lately is a kind of awakening in which I fully accept the inconsistencies of my life along with the eccentric tendencies. I am no longer irritated if somebody thinks I am "odd" or "different" or "unusual." With the French I say, "Vive la difference." If I am a misfit, so what?

One might ask how accurate the word "misfit" is when I use it to describe myself. The dictionary definition is, "unable to adjust to one's circumstances or considered disturbingly different." These words have applied to me throughout my life and it used to bother me. Now I say, "Whatever other people think of me is none of my business."

This also applies to my first love, my own writing. If you like it, fine; if you don't, that's okay. I write the way I write and that's all there is to it. It's a free country...so far.

As the comic strip character Popeye used to say, "I am what I am." The Lord in Heaven has a similar description of himself, "I Am Who Am." And sometimes he just describes himself as "I Am."

As for me, a child of God, I am in the world but not of the world. I come from some other place and will return to some other place. So just consider me a visitor here. That's enough for me. If I am thought to be a misfit here, okay. I would rather be a misfit than be considered "normal" or "average."

Words obviously have limitations but I still enjoy playing with them. They make good companions. In just a few words I can say without hesitation, I am an orphan and I am a misfit. I used to think that was a problem. Now I think the orphan/misfit description of myself is more healthy than qualifying for the word "normal" which in our world can be equated with "insane" or at the very least, "impaired."

Here is a question for you about some other important words: Is society a place of coercive conformity or is it a place where it is acceptable for diverse individuals to freely gather, based on one or more things they have in common?

My own response as a freedom loving Aquarian-Contrarian is that society is only an abstraction and should not operate like a prison. In a real sense, society does not exist except as an abstraction. Sociology, despite its pretensions, is a soft inconclusive science. So is psychology.

I studied philosophy and psychology at depth with the Jesuits at Boston College. Also, I delved into educational psychology at Boston University Graduate School.

Eventually, I taught logic and philosophy at New Hampshire College. I came to believe that those subjects are multi-faceted and expansive, not limited or restrictive. Ditto for the human being with an individual personality.

So please don't expect me to be too logical. Life, I believe, is filled with contradictions and paradoxes. The contradictions and paradoxes of life have always been key elements of my journey toward higher consciousness. Those tendencies have found a home in my psyche as well as in the world of seemingly random circumstances outside of me.

When one idea is opposed to another it's a contradiction. A paradox is a seeming contradiction that may have some truth in it. A paradox, according to a Zen interpretation, is a truth standing on its head trying to get our attention.

Mrs. White hated to be contradicted and I never heard her use the word "paradox." As for me, I greatly enjoy mysteries and paradoxes. Maybe that's because I have often felt as if I were a visitor from some other location in space.

I once thought I came from another planet and arrived here by mistake; now I think my origin was in another galaxy. Was it a mistake to come here for a temporary transitional existence on Earth? No.

I might have had alien thoughts at certain times, but now I believe my time here was part of God's plan for part of my eternal life. It was something I needed to experience.

For example, I had to experience life as a Catholic Charities kid with Mrs. White before returning to Granny's duplex. One of the benefits of living for nine years with Mrs. White was that afterwards I would never take my freedom lightly. I would be true to myself after leaving Norwood.

Freedom? Obviously, I never felt free at Mrs. White's. For me, there was a feeling of claustrophobic and oppressive unreality in that environment. The house resembled a high class detention center where I lived in first class accommodations.

Nevertheless, detention is imprisonment. The environment itself was not the problem. With Mrs. White I received the best food, clothing and shelter prior to deportation to the country where I originated. I was waiting year after year for the delayed freedom that would greet me at Granny's where I had once lived in a spirit of freedom.

In 1946 when I moved in with Granny O'Connell on her side of the duplex next to the East Dedham Railroad Station in the blighted part of town I finally had my freedom. My freedom, however, was accompanied by deficits in food, clothing and shelter.

My food was at malnutrition level. My clothing deteriorated steadily with time as I resorted to patches on every item that I wore, from underwear to jackets. The shelter provided by the duplex was substandard compared to the meticulously maintained middle class colonial home where I had lived with Mrs. White for nine years.

What is a duplex? For those who are not familiar with duplexes I will give you a brief explanation. A duplex is in some ways similar to a row house but there might be a variety in styles of row houses whereas each side of a true duplex is the mirror image of the unit on the opposite side.

Picture a house divided in two from top to bottom and set up with the same amount of space on each side. The floor plans of each side's living space are identical reverse images and the rooms are all the same size as their opposites.

In Granny's house you entered at the front where two main doorways stood side by side. If you opened the door to your left you went into 22 Walnut Place where I lived.

If you then looked to the left you would see a door leading to the front room, also known as the parlor. If you looked straight ahead you saw a flight of stairs leading up to the second floor with its bedrooms and bath.

Upstairs to the left there were two bedrooms, one a moderate size and the other tiny. Both bedrooms had extremely sloped ceilings that had to be carefully avoided if one preferred not to develop a flattened skull.

If you opened the door at the top of the stairs you would see the bathroom that was shared by both sides of the duplex. On the other side of the wall to the right of the stairs was a matching door for the other family's entrance to the bath.

The bathroom was the only room in the house that was used by both families. It contained one ancient white bathtub with badly stained enamel, one toilet with badly stained enamel and a flush box with pull chain up above it, and one tiny sink with badly stained enamel.

The only source of light was a very low watt bulb. Although there was a skylight I never thought of it as a source of light. It was so covered with railroad soot the daylight outside could not break through and illuminate the bathroom. Neither could anybody loosen the window's rusty hinges and expect to allow some outside air to filter inside.

Am I saying that upstairs in Granny's duplex there was only one bathroom with one tub and one toilet to serve my Uncle Bill and his wife and several kids next door plus me and whoever else was living on Granny's side at the time? That's what I'm saying.

In addition, the bathroom was unheated because there was no central heating in the house. Upstairs in the house there was no source of heat to be found except for some rusty and dust laden floor vents that allowed a small supply of heat to rise slowly from the first floor and up into the two upstairs bedrooms and the bath.

In each of the duplex apartments there were two sources of heat downstairs to heat each home. A large iron oil stove heated the kitchen and part of the small dining room next to the kitchen. An inefficient kerosene space heater with no vent, and therefore very hazardous, was located in the parlor or "front room" next to the front window.

These sources of heat functioned only in the winter months. Along with the negligible amount of heat upstairs in winter there would be a layer of ice on each of the windows. So you might say it was like living in an old fashioned "ice box" because inside a "refrigerator" would be warmer.

During the rest of the year the house was heated only by Mother Nature. To deal with extremes of heat we had damaged screens on the ancient windows. Some of the window panes were cracked and stayed that way for decades.

Downstairs the rooms were in one row, with parlor in the front, dining room in the middle, and kitchen out back with a pantry off the kitchen. In the kitchen a tall hot water tank stood directly beside the huge black cast iron Magee stove on its claw legs. Since the stove only functioned during the winter there was no hot water in faucets from April or May to October or November, depending on the weather.

In the cooler weather the large kitchen stove provided heat plus hot water for the tank. During the warmer weather when the large cast iron stove was not used, a two-burner kerosene "hot plate" was plunked on top of the iron stove.

If you needed hot water to shave at the kitchen sink you heated it on top of the stove. Most of the year, if you wanted a warm bath upstairs you heated kettles of water on the little kerosene stove or the large cast iron stove and carried the water upstairs to the bath to mix it with cold tap water until you reached a bath water temperature you could tolerate.

Off the kitchen on each side of the duplex was a long unheated enclosed porch. Granny's porch was where she tended to her many plants that wintered indoors. Also, in the porch was a surplus U.S. Army cot with flat springs. I used it on hot summer nights when the tiny upstairs bedroom with one window was too hot to endure.

From age fourteen and beyond, "comfort" was not part of my life at Granny's house. But, as the old saying cautions: "Beggars can't be choosers." Neither can orphans.

Yes, I was still the orphan even though I avoided attaching that description to myself until recently. Even if I didn't adopt that way of describing myself, I now realize that being an orphan has always been my permanent condition.

Although sometimes my status seemed to change, underneath the surface as well as on the surface I was still the orphan. After all, I had the status of an orphan. Until age 21 if anything disabled the adult who was allegedly caring for my needs I would instantly become a ward of the State.

When I was young the age of maturity was 21. Until 21 our rights were limited. Youths were not completely free. For example, it was illegal for us to drink alcohol.

Starting in 1946, after leaving Mrs. White's, I was living with my father and grandmother. But I knew as a daily reality that if anything happened to them the Commonwealth of Massachusetts would decide on my destiny.

The State would be my caretaker and I would lose the freedom I had gained on my departure from Norwood. The very thought of this idea was too grim to think about.

From the State's viewpoint I now had a family. But from my point of view, once an orphan, always an orphan. At first when I moved into Granny's side of her duplex I felt as if I finally had a real family. But how real was it?

I was only remotely connected with Granny because of the age gap. And my connection with my father was even more remote. Although we now lived in the same house, we had little in common.

Emotionally, when I moved into 22 Walnut Place I initially believed I no longer had to avoid answering questions about where I lived or with whom. I could state, "I live with my father and grandmother on Walnut Place in East Dedham." That would do it, right?

No, it did not do it. I soon learned that escape from my reality was not possible. When I mentioned my father and grandmother, the door was immediately opened for curious people to ask about the rest of my reality. For example, "What about your mother?"

Having a missing mother was beyond explanation. She was not dead but she was absent. When I learned why she was absent I was deeply ashamed of that burdensome truth. Could I explain her absence? No.

I could neither erase her existence nor escape her reality. Nor could I talk about her. The emotional pain was too overwhelming to discuss the situation with anybody.

Because of the shame surrounding her insanity, I could not say, "My mother is in an insane asylum." It was hard to even think it, never mind say it. But I had learned years before to respond to questions about her by saying without hesitation, "I lost her when I was little."

That response was too vague. "How did you lose her?" I could not answer that question. So I would clam up. And people were never satisfied with my silence.

Eventually, in self-defense, I had to make the leap to saying, "She's dead." I hated lying but that usually stopped the questions. However, my claim that she was dead did not stop the emotional turmoil her condition as an inmate in a State insane asylum stirred up in my psyche.

That fact seemed so shameful and fearful to me that I would not speak about it to even my closest friends. How could I tell them I had an insane mother who was locked up in a fearful asylum? How could I tell them I had not seen her since infancy?

To me, the truth about my life sounded more like horror fiction than fact. How could I ever reveal this terrible truth? If people knew about her, wouldn't they think I might have inherited her insanity? Wouldn't they wonder if I might flip my own lid someday and go haywire?

When I learned about her situation and where she was located it added another item to my reality of being "different" from other boys. Not only was I a Catholic Charities kid who was abandoned by my own family; I also had been born to a woman declared insane and locked up because she might be a hazard to herself and others.

I cannot overemphasize the strangeness of never seeing my mother since infancy yet knowing she was a few miles away in a State hospital for the insane. It was a fact that could not be discussed. It was taboo. I couldn't even permit myself to think about it.

The situation was truly unthinkable. It was the stuff of frequent nightmares. I had many of those that could have provided plots for horror movies. I would often wake up in the middle of the night trembling and screaming but unable to discuss the vivid nightmare scenes about my mother.

As I look back at the early decades of my life it becomes readily apparent to me that I was always leading a double life. I was carrying massive secrets that were very important for me to hide. So I had an impenetrable secret self.

I also had a social self in which I only partially revealed personal information to those closest to me. That is, if I could trust them. Trust was always an issue for me. Actually, nobody earned my complete trust. How could they?

I had been betrayed and abandoned too often to give total trust to anyone. My trust was always conditional. Everybody around me had a status similar to "on probation." So it did not take much abuse or neglect for me to remove my trust.

Obviously, I had only limited trust in the members of my family of origin, the O'Connells. Although I was just a few miles away at Mrs. White's only one aunt and uncle came to visit me a few times during my nine years in Norwood.

So I became an expert in the art of playing the role of the outsider. After all, the whole O'Connell group had taken part in a conspiracy of silence in which nobody had revealed the truth to me about my mother's condition. As a group, my own close relatives intensified my outsider status.

When I visited Granny periodically on short vacations, if relatives came to visit, they maintained their silence. I can understand that now. After all, they lived by "Mind your own business" which was the slogan of that era. But later when family members began to talk about my mother's insanity more openly it was shocking to realize how many people had known the truth and withheld it from me.

I had heard indirect comments about "Margaret" from Granny O'Connell every so often when I visited 22 Walnut Place in East Dedham as a boy. But I had never received any meaningful anecdotes about my mother's life before she had plunged into the mental abyss.

After my move to Walnut Place at age 14, once in a while

my father would sit with me in Granny's parlor and deliver a five or ten minute monologue about my absent mother. He would tell me how nice she was "before she went."

Although I sat in rapt attention when this happened, I asked no questions. I remained frozen in place. His monologues terrified me and I always anxiously waited for him to conclude his remarks.

I was still "the quiet one." The silent observer. The outsider. The listener who said very little.

Actually, nobody in those days was comfortable with admitting that a family member was insane. It was a subject avoided at all costs by members of the O'Connell clan except on rare occasions when Granny would mention Margaret in one of her storytelling monologue sessions.

Granny had a knack for the dramatic oral approach to life and her voice would have projected well on a Broadway stage. When she mentioned my mother and used the words "before she went" as my father did, Granny would point at her own head to illustrate how Margaret "went."

Come to think of it, in my nine years at Mrs. White's house I don't recall anybody ever mentioning my mother. Mrs. White never talked about the parents or other relatives of us boys. It was as if they did not exist. There was an unspoken code of privacy in that house. Privacy by omission.

The only exception was the Catholic Charities social worker whom I overheard talking with Mrs. White about my mother when the social worker was on a periodic visit.

That was how I learned the truth about why my mother was absent from my life. I was supposed to be in bed when the social worker visited but I had a need to go from the third floor bedroom to the bathroom on the second floor.

At that location I could hear the voices in the parlor. After I heard the social worker talking about my mother's status in "the asylum," I soon looked up that word in my dictionary.

That's how the truth about my mother emerged.

The new knowledge about her location left me so terrified that from that time onward I would never even consider asking a question about my mother to Mrs. White or anybody else. To me, that would be like opening Pandora's box of horrors.

Besides, I was in a house where questions were unwelcome and I was well trained in the practice of asking no questions. The boys who lived at Mrs. White's kept their questions to the barest minimum.

"May I get up from the table now?" "May I go to the bathroom?" "May I go upstairs and read?" It was clear to us that any really personal questions at Mrs. White's were very unwelcome and should be carefully avoided. We might be severely punished for asking.

It is no exaggeration to state that an integral part of Mrs. White's way of life was her careful avoidance of answering questions. To her, I believe any question was similar to a contradiction. And she passionately hated to be contradicted.

She avoided volunteering information about her own history and about the families of all six of us boys. She had her own personal code of silence. And it was contagious.

We boys avoided asking personal questions to each other as well. If one of us did this, the other boy was likely to say, "M.Y.O.B." meaning "Mind your own business." We might say, "That's for me to know and for you to guess." Or we might say, "Ask me no questions and I'll tell you no lies."

As for our guardian, she focused her attention on the task at hand and hated to be sidetracked, especially by questions. The more personal the question might be, the more unwelcome it would be for Mrs. White.

Have I made it clear that for me and everyone around me, the less said the better? We were a large and quiet household most of the time.

Like many families we lived very private lives as far as the outside world was concerned. At home, were we more open? Did we share our deepest feelings? No, we did not.

After all, our feelings were nobody else's business. We were living in an age when personal privacy was maintained by most people. People went out of their way to avoid being intrusive even though they might be curious.

Averse to questions, Mrs. White would not even honor such an intrusion with a clear answer. If you dared ask, she would say in her Irish accent with a toss of her head, "Sure and I don't know" or "Faith, it's none of my business, is it?"

Then Mrs. White would change the subject instantly as she brushed off the query. She never talked about her husband's death or her own past. Neither did the six of us boys talk about our pasts, nor did Mr. Vincent the boarder.

Those who have gone on a silent spiritual retreat would get some idea of the way we lived most of the time. The house full of about a dozen people at 42 Mountain Avenue in Norwood contained the same kind of silence as a monastery or church or library in the old days.

Today the world I live in seems to be immersed in noise. I can't even listen to my favorite radio talk shows without the interruptions of extremely loud and fast talking announcers spouting their commercials and shouting phone numbers four and five times. I am so grateful that I can retreat from this by shutting the radio off and working quietly on my latest book.

The code of silence at 42 Mountain Avenue in Norwood did not have to be announced. It was part of the way of life. Mrs. White was the opposite of Granny when it came to sharing information about her past. Granny's past was a dramatic monologue. Mrs. White's was a closed and locked book. She lived and worked in the present tense.

My father was also averse to questions about the past because the past stirred up such painful memories for him.

So I learned to just listen when information flowed from him about family realities that had an impact on me. Why ask him a question when the answer would probably be a piece of defensive fiction? He tended to exaggerate or minimize.

I can see now that I had some compassion for my father. Knowing that truth brought him intense pain, I figured it was natural for him to dodge it. And I tried not to be intrusive.

For the most part, when I spent time with him he only talked about sensitive subjects when under the influence of alcohol. "*In vino veritas*." That was when I listened very carefully and learned some of the facts about myself.

His way of dodging truthful comments about his personal history was to deliver a monologue in his own method of providing a story with no focus and lacking a conclusion.

In personal conversations with curious people I often did something similar. I did not want to stir up a rambling vague lecture. So when I was around Fred I kept my questions to a minimum just as I had with Mrs. White.

In fact, I even had a strategy for dealing with information that came from him. "Divide by two or multiply by two." My father suffered from both overstating and understating. He was not the only one who did this. He had this tendency in common with minority populations throughout the world.

Giving clear, direct answers to questions could jeopardize the lives of minority people whether they might be African, Irish, or some other ethnic classification. They became adept at dodging comments that might lead them toward hazardous consequences. A wrong reply meant big trouble.

Why risk an honest answer? Why not lie? Or evade? In the United States we have such tendencies at the highest levels of our government. Evasion of the truth, or distortion of it, are ways of life for many of our esteemed leaders.

This evasive approach was especially true of the Irish who were subjugated by the British for some 700 years.

Having been victims of British deceit and outright lies, assassinations and genocide for centuries, the Irish felt no guilt when they provided indirect responses to questions.

There is even a bit of British humor about this tendency. "You Irish never give direct answers to questions. You always answer a question with another question."

Irish response: "Who told you that?"

Looking at my life objectively, I can say that I was a slowly recovering introvert who took decades to learn to be more extroverted and open about personal information. I was frustrated by questions during much of my life and used to do my best to dance around the offending queries.

My Irish heritage may have been a factor. But I think the important factor was the shame my past inflicted on me. My psychological wounds were so deep I preferred to keep them to myself. So I would choose denial or minimization.

As "the quiet one" I often blushed and chose silence instead of communication. Not that I had nothing to say. My silence meant I was terrified of the potential negative feedback I might trigger by being open and forthright. I could be open with my close companions at times, but ordinarily I protected myself from harm by choosing silence.

My own distaste for personal questions was just as extreme as Mrs. White's and my father's until I reached middle age. Then I became more open with people due to individual and group therapy. For much of my earlier adult life I'm surprised that people didn't describe me as Tom the Dodger. It would have been an apt description.

Among my most effective responses to direct personal questions were "Why are you asking that question?" or "How am I supposed to know the answer to that?" Or I might just give a wide eyed look accompanied by silence and a shrug. Like an apprentice, I had learned from experts how to dodge questions. So I became an expert too.

Chapter 6
Dedham High School

My teenage life in East Dedham at Granny O'Connell's duplex began early in September of 1946. Having enjoyed my summer of total freedom in the Adirondacks, I moved into the tiny bedroom occupied by my bachelor Uncle Joe whenever he returned home from Washington, D.C. where he held clerical jobs in federal agencies.

I was now a temporary occupant of Joe's room with its single window. Again, as had been the case at Mrs. White's, I had no specific rights. At Granny's house, I was an outsider living once again as a guest, as I had been at age 5 before being relocated from Granny's to Mrs. White's.

At Mrs. White's I had always been a temporary occupant on loan from Catholic Charities. At Granny's, Uncle Joe had his own bedroom, the smaller one. My father Fred had his own room too, the larger one. Fred was the oldest son.

Unlike Mrs. White's, we didn't have inner spring mattresses in those days at Granny's place. The mattresses were thin and sometimes you could feel the flat springs underneath your rear end or sticking into your ribs.

Granny slept on a flat spring surplus U.S. Army cot next to the kitchen in the dining room that was never used as a dining room. In addition, there was a large dining table there that was never used for dining. Also in the dining room there was a cumbersome piece of very dysfunctional furniture that was described as a "buffet" but never used for a buffet.

An antique furniture dealer would often stop by and try to persuade her to sell him some pieces, but Granny would always say no. His pitches did not work with her.

As far as I can recall, nobody ever explained the system of bedroom occupation. This was consistent with the general behavior of adults in those times. The adults believed there was never any need to explain anything to a younger person.

With no explanation, I would have what seemed to be my own private room for months. Then suddenly Joe would show up and I would move to my father's room to share his double bed if he happened to be there. If he was elsewhere I would sleep by myself in his double bed. And that was that.

I changed nothing in Joe's room. His sepia high school graduating class photo stayed on the wall next to the small closet. His locked World War II Army trunk of personal stuff stayed exactly where it was on the floor in the closet.

Also, I changed nothing in my father's room. I used it as I found it and that was all. I believe this led to a life-long habit of leaving most things exactly where I found them. This behavior was reinforced by Mrs.White's dictum: "A place for everything and everything in its place."

Having a few days at my disposal before school started in September, I filled the time with books borrowed from the Dedham Public Library and its East Dedham branch. This gave me enough books to read before school began.

I was entering my sophomore year at Dedham High, a four-year high school where I would bypass the freshman year. I had completed the Norwood school system's three-year junior high and in my next classes at Norwood I would have been a high school sophomore. So I was destined never to be a high school freshman.

Based on my grades in Norwood I was slated for the B College Division in Dedham, not the A Division. And I did not mind this at all. I had chosen to be a B student at Norwood Junior High because I wanted to be average.

I knew the A Division at Dedham High was an endurance test and I was not interested in extra stress. In fact, I was looking forward to sophomore year as one long vacation with a minimum of pressure and a maximum of freedom.

After being released from Mrs. White's restrictive environment I was engulfed in a kind of free flowing intoxication. The most exhilarating intoxicant was the fact that I was now entirely free to be me, whoever that might be.

Who on Earth could tell what my real self should be? I remained very confused by my painful early abandonment experiences over which I had no control. So it was only natural that I would ask myself, "Who am I?"

My exploration into this mystery would turn out to be one of the major preoccupations of my life. "Who am I?" "Why did I not start out with a stable existence in a dependable family setting?" "Why am I here on the planet Earth?"

I was always haunted by questions: "Why did God allow me to be uprooted from the only family I had ever felt comfortable with?" "Why did God let my only brother die?" "Why did I have to be a motherless kid?"

Questions, questions. But silence from the Lord. Yet I never stopped believing in God. I am still grateful for Mrs. White's intense interest in our Catholic religion. She was thorough and devoted in her religious practice. Because of her ferocious domination at 42 Mountain Avenue, the Irish widow was a powerful spiritual role model.

Oddly, I think my search for my true self began to be energized at Dedham High in sophomore year as I devoted myself to having fun in class as well as away from school.

During classes, especially English classes, I released the offbeat sense of humor that had been imprisoned in Mrs. White's fundamentally serious household. Now it was as if the nine years of humor that had been held back most of the time came bouncing forth into open space, propelled by my freedom loving unconscious mind.

English teachers were the most lenient, so that's where I did my best to entertain myself and my classmates. Most of my humorous outbursts were based on playing with words the teacher had used. Trying to be funny, I would put another twist on their meaning.

This brought laughs but also placed me in that after school mode called "detention." And it gave me low grades in conduct on report cards. But I did not care. "Who cares?"

Diffidence and indifference provided my mindset as a high school sophomore recently freed from the harsh discipline of Margaret Monahan White. Now I had no limits or boundaries. I was free to be myself…whatever that meant.

The brief version of my years at Dedham High is found in the following sentences. Although inwardly anxious I worked at giving an impression of great calmness. This served as a defense against those who might wish to intrude into my inner consciousness and my disturbing family realities. I became a skilled silent defender of my privacy.

Also, I began a return to my earlier mode of making choices that might be helpful to me. My grades improved slightly and I became interested in creating an athletic achievement of some kind. My Chemistry teacher, also the track coach, thought my tall and extremely thin frame would be an excellent addition to his team. He was wrong.

I went out for track but I quickly dropped the track team. The pains in my chest and other parts of my thin body were too terrifying. Instead I joined the golf team because golf was usually painless. Also, I had practically been raised on Norfolk Golf Course. And it was my kind of slow game.

I paid the price for quitting the track team because I had the coach for Chemistry for the rest of the year. Over and over he cast aspersions about "quitters" and made sure he was staring at me each time he said that word. Looking back, I see his behavior as a clever form of verbal abuse.

After my sophomore year in vacation mode with my place on the golf team and my quest for fun and laughter, I decided in my junior year to buckle down and be an Honor Roll student. Actually, it had been difficult for me to pretend I was only an average student. I was a natural when it came to learning, studying and testing.

Now I recaptured my focus and was college bound. So term after term I was on the Honor Roll. This meant I would have no trouble qualifying for Boston College. In my mind there was no other college, just BC. I was determined to go there no matter what, regardless of my money deficit.

There certainly was a money deficit. Near the end of my junior year of high school my father and a colleague at Dedham Post Office decided to move to Maine together to start a new business. So Fred escaped the security of the Post Office, pooled funds with Hazel, departed from Granny's place, and left me alone and penniless with Granny.

Fred and Hazel were virtually married except for the fact that Fred had not formally divorced my insane mother. This was a complication that would be resolved much later. First, the two were going to enter a partnership that involved setting up a motor court with 10 prefabricated cottages on Route One in the seaside community of Wells, Maine.

To make this possible, it took all of Hazel's savings and every cent my father could extract from Granny, including money she had set aside to help me with my future college education. Fred had no savings of his own. He could not enter an enterprise unless he had other people's money at his disposal. So he put his powers of persuasion to work.

His departure while I was still in high school was one more proof that my situation was not near the top of my father's priority list. But I did not hate him for his concentration on his own personal survival.

After all, he was my only available parent and I believed in the commandment Honor thy Father and Mother. However, when one has an absent insane mother and a constantly disappearing father some adjustments to this commandment might have been in order.

Order? In those days my mind was as much in the world of imagination as it was in the world of order and logic. It still is. Also, as I have noted before, I was aware of how my father had suffered from the loss of my mother to insanity and the loss of my little brother Jackie to pneumonia. Hadn't Fred earned the right to develop the plot for his own life story instead of settling for someone else's interpretation?

Since there is usually a good side and a negative side to each life experience, the good news for me was that after he abandoned me once again I was as free as a young man could possibly be. A loss often turns out to be a gain, as the Chinese philosopher Lao Tzu made very clear.

Not that I had ever completely submitted to Fred O'Connell's authority anyhow. Nor had he shown any great interest in having parental authority over me. He was plenty busy with his own life. That gave me more freedom.

In Granny's house my father and I were like two boats in the same harbor passing each other often but doing very little communicating. Just waves of hands and nods of the head as we each sailed in our own direction. That was about it.

He was up at 6a.m. and off to the Post Office whereas I was a later sleeper. So we rarely had meals together. In the evening I would be at the Dedham Library or the pool room with my friends. My father would always be elsewhere.

That was okay by me. Our private lives were our own business. I never asked him questions about his life and he seldom asked me questions about mine.

I rarely had real conversations with my father. He tended to talk in paragraphs and I usually responded with single sentences or just a couple of words. As I've said before, I rarely asked questions about his activities. And I had no interest in telling him about myself and my pals.

To find the right words to describe how we related to each

other is difficult. But probably the most honest view as I look back at my high school years is that we were not just acting like strangers, we actually were strangers. We didn't really know each other.

There was a serious intimacy deficit. A very thick psychological wall existed between us and I was emotionally incapable of changing the situation. Based on the extremes of abandonment that I had suffered from his decisions about my life, there was a strong undercurrent of suppressed anger against him in my spirit.

I had always been the quiet boy at Mrs. White's. I was still the quiet boy in Granny's house even though I was more and more sociable at school and with my pals.

My father probably did his best to break through my silence at times but how could he accomplish that feat with me? Silence was my habitual lifestyle preference. Also, I used silence for a self-protective shield to avoid new wounds that would overlay all the old ones.

Without having a real understanding in those days about Posttraumatic Stress Disorder, I was a living example of PTSD. To cope with it, I had developed many layers of defensive silence. Some of it was innate. Much was added as a conscious strategy to deal with a world where devastating unexpected attacks seemed bound to come my way.

A lot of my silence was probably unconscious self-medication to strengthen my spirit in the face of life-threatening events. The world as I saw it was not a happy peaceful place. In a world that threatened me cruelly I was not likely to see life as a happy or peaceful state of existence.

I have a friend who enjoys saying that he thinks the universe is friendly. Based on my experiences I think otherwise. I think the universe has erratic moods that might qualify for a definition based on the mental health category that used to be known as manic depressive disorder.

Over and over in my life, destiny linked to the moods of the universe seemed to hit me below the belt. Ouch! So I became hyper alert. You might call me defensive or even "super-sensitive." Or how about the term I came up with to describe myself a few years ago? "Exquisitely sensitive."

As for day to day existence with my father, at Granny's we continued to live uncomfortably under the same roof until his escape to Maine. I'm sure the discomfort for both of us at Walnut Place was psychological as well as environmental.

A very deep alienation had taken root in my connection to him on the day he dropped me off at Mrs. White's house at age five. At that age I had already experienced a fragmented life and one abandonment after another. However, the betrayal at age five after being led to believe I had a permanent home with Granny was an awful psychic wound. This was truly a life-changing psychological event.

When I was a young boy at Mrs. White's, whenever Fred came to Norwood to take me for a ride to visit my family in Dedham I would usually become ill. Part of the nausea problem was from cigars he often smoked. Another part was a negative gut reaction to the parent who stayed remotely connected to me but avoided a consistent loving relationship.

In my senior year of Dedham High I only saw Fred on his periodic visits when he came down from Maine. And the idea of calling him Dad still seemed totally bizarre.

I had decided not to call him Dad at age five after he dropped me off at the Catholic Charities home run by Mrs. White. So omitting "Dad" was a deeply entrenched habit.

As years passed I still avoided calling him Dad except on rare occasions. If I were writing him a letter the words "Dear Dad" would be in the salutation and that would be that.

When I wrote to him that way it was as if I were dealing with a fictional character created by the pen of Charles Dickens. Fred Who? What was his connection to me? He had usually been missing when I needed him. Throughout my life I felt that our true relationship was more fiction than fact.

As my father and I grew older I still could neither call him Dad nor could I fake a smile in his presence. When he smiled at me with genuine warmth my response was just a neutral look. To put it clearly, I was always in a state of impending terror when I had to spend time with him.

To add to the problem, I was so self-conscious that I was reluctant to show my crooked teeth. I am not exaggerating when I state that it must have been very painful emotionally for Fred to try to break through my shield of silence.

He was the extrovert who had spent his adult life being very friendly with the people at the customer side of his Post Office window. I was the fundamental introvert. For me, the less conversation the better. We were polar opposites.

As I reflect on my father's life and mine in this story that includes some observations about the two of us, I am trying to come to grips with realities that part of me would just as soon avoid. But I have decided in this memoir not to create any dead end streets. I am not dodging reality here.

Deep inside I had an insightful spirit that had always seen him as a threat, for good reasons. His decisions had placed me in situations I found traumatic even though I did not know the meaning of that word until a few decades ago.

Obviously, I had a natural tendency to avoid being friendly with people who threatened my existence or short circuited my goals. In spite of the fact that he was my father, he was one of those people. I did not feel friendly near him.

Actually, I have never been very good at covering up uncomfortable feelings by pretending to be happy. I still can't. My facial expression has to match my inner feelings. In playing my roles in life I have not been a good actor. When I tried to act "as if," it did not work for me. I have always had a deep need to be authentic and true to myself.

Despite the emotional distancing that engulfed my psyche when Fred was around, I want to state that I did appreciate any efforts he made to show concern for my well-being.

Objectively, I can say that he never completely abandoned me. He only partially abandoned me, on a fairly regular basis, providing intermittent emotional torture.

Actually, in spite of the terror of Mrs.White's wrath and her violent disposition she was one of the most consistent people I have ever known. I was well provided for by her during my nine-year Catholic Charities experience.

Later, on his visits during the years when I lived alone with Granny on her side of the duplex, my father would make gestures such as passing on some of his old clothes to me when I reached his size. I did not mind that at all. I was not difficult to please. I appreciated his interest.

Also, to make sure I didn't starve he often came down from Maine and dropped off a case of canned vegetables, such as diced carrots and peas. I liked plain canned peas best and have never lost my taste for them. Forget the carrots. Once in a while he would deliver a case of Dinty Moore's Beef Stew. For me, this was a protein delicacy.

Often, in a burst of generosity he would grab the magical wad of bills that would always be in his pocket, and he would peel off some tens and fives and put them in my hand. I would always thank him sincerely for the money which would usually be invested in getting some sorely needed clothing such as socks and underwear.

Over the years he also gave me valuable sheets of new postage stamps. They were for my collection that eventually disappeared years later when I was in the U.S. Army.

There might also be some trivial conversation with my father during his visits. But for the sake of accuracy, let me just emphasize that I habitually shut down emotionally whenever he was around.

I did not intentionally shut down. It was an automatic response. And I am sure he must have been baffled by my behavior. Anyone would have been.

In those days I did not know what was going on with me psychologically. After all, I was an orphan and a misfit and was not in touch with those realities.

As I look back, it is clear now that when my father showed up there was an inner darkness in me that emerged from its hiding place in my unconscious mind. It was the source of my extremely realistic nightmares. It had an ominous aspect and afflicted my spirit painfully.

I possessed a challenging combination of dutiful love for the man who was my father coupled with deep estrangement. But he was my father no matter what. Knowing he cared about me to some degree, I appreciated his connection with my life even though it was inconsistent. Yet our personal history was a barrier to warm intimacy.

Let's face it; I did not trust him. How could I? I can see now that I was better off psychologically when he was at a distance even if that caused some nutrition problems for me.

But positive action is better than whining and complaining. I came from a time in history when complaining was considered a vice. We were not "entitled" to anything at all. Zilch. Nothing. Zero.

So I acted to offset my borderline starvation at Granny's. I took a part-time job at The Four Hundred, a soda fountain snack bar in Dedham Square across from the bicycle shop where a local "myth" told of other covert activities there.

At The Four Hundred I could nibble on Peggy Lawton's brownies and date bars and treat myself to ice cream sundaes and banana splits. I could also give large portions of ice cream to my pals when they dropped by. That's what I did.

I knew at that time that it was up to me to shape my own destiny. Who else was going to do it for me? So, in my senior year at Dedham High in 1948-49 I became motivated to express my love of words and expand my vocabulary by entering the Boston Herald Traveler's spelling contest.

I had won all the spelling bees when I was in elementary school. Why couldn't I be victorious again if I set my mind to it? So I set my mind to the task. By immersing myself in the work of studying enormous sheets of unfamiliar words I memorized the spelling of thousands of words.

Then I faced the daunting process of eliminating other contestants in front of large audiences. In spite of my terror of performing in front of the huge audience of students in the auditorium at Dedham High, I won the competition locally and was named Senior Class Champion. Somewhere in my files I still have the impressive medals.

However, when I faced the pressure of being on the stage in the final spelling bee at Boston Public Library my neurotic introversion was too much for me. I flunked on a very easy word and for the rest of my life I forgot to remember what that word was. My embarrassment was horrendous.

My self-consciousness was extreme. I was not only an unusually shy introvert but a high anxiety introvert. This was a hindrance in the spelling competition and an obstacle later in any activity involving public performance.

An example was my small part in the Dedham High Senior Class Play. I only had a couple of lines to memorize and enjoyed being part of the cast as "a derelict" with a blacked out tooth. But being on a stage in front of a large crowd would get my heart racing at twice the normal speed.

The extreme self-consciousness was a fundamental aspect of my personality for a very long time. It might have seemed to others that when I was an adult I overcame it, but that conclusion was based on erroneous logic.

Just because I appeared to be calm and did many activities that brought attention to me in front of all kinds of crowds in large lecture halls and auditoriums did not mean that the terror of being scrutinized by others had been extinguished.

As an adult, my terror followed me like a threatening PTSD shadow and was often accompanied by chronic fatigue. Maybe my inner tension created much of the fatigue.

Certainly the secret life of having a missing mother in a State insane asylum provided ongoing stress based on the terror that somebody might reveal my secret publicly. I knew how people felt about any family that had insanity which required placement in a State institution. It was a stigma of mammoth proportions. An unspeakable stigma. My stigma.

Moving slowly became my personal pattern. At Norwood Junior High the gym teacher called me Old Man O'Connell because of my physical slowness. And the more he called me that the slower I got.

Now I fit his description better. I'm an old man and I still have my own pace. It's not fast. Luckily, my mind is fast but not my body. My energy is slow energy when it comes to bodily exertion and fast when it comes to mental activity.

With my close friends I was distracted from the chronic shyness and fatigue. I was the same way with my family. But elsewhere the dark shadow of exquisite sensitivity stuck to me as a trigger for emotional and nervous system reactions, especially when facing overwhelming stress.

My sensitivity always escalated in noisy or overly bright environments. Some people love bright sun shining on them or bright lights glowing around them. I don't.

Mrs. White's house had always been aglow but I adjusted pretty well to the environment there. The lighting in our third floor bedroom next to the attic was moderate. But when all the lights in the house were blazing, her place had been similar to a lighthouse visible to all ships at sea.

Life with Granny from age 14 to 21 was like living in a dark cave where only one or two incandescent low watt bulbs shed their light. To this day I am sensitive to bright light and make the following quip: "I was raised in a cave with wolves, so glare is a problem for me."

Crowds are a problem too. I am likely to avoid parades, even though I gladly attended when my kids were young. Actually, I am not sure whether my sensitivity to light and my aversion to loud noise and crowds came through my conditioning or might have been in my DNA. Probably both.

I remember that when I was quite little, my father engaged in one of his periodic attempts to act like a father. He took me to the deafening Ringling Brothers Barnum & Bailey Circus in Boston Garden. The building was huge and so was the crowd. I was intimidated by both of these factors.

I have always disliked crowds and their stampeding boisterous herd mentality. I became more intimidated by the noisy circus crowd when they shot a silver clad man from a loud cannon into mid-air and into a net many yards away.

The moment the boom hit my ears and the man went flying through the air like a missile I started to scream. I would not stop screaming until my father picked me up and carried me to the street outside Boston Garden.

Naturally, my father never took me to another circus. Instead, as I grew older he sometimes would take me to Suffolk Downs for the horse races that he loved so much. I didn't like the noisy gambling crowds there but I enjoyed the exciting horse races at Suffolk.

Also, on rare occasions my father took me to Boston Braves and Red Sox baseball games. I could cope with the noise of the baseball crowds. And I enjoyed seeing some of the well known players such as Jimmie Foxx in action. Of all the sports that are available on TV I prefer baseball or golf.

I give my father credit for these attempts to bond with me to some degree. But even at a young age, because of the various acts of abandonment inflicted on me in my earliest years I could never fully relax in my father's company.

In a burst of candor when I was an adult and he was sipping on rum and coke, my father revealed a key aspect of our father-son relationship. He confessed that over the years he had experienced great difficulty spending time with me, especially when I was young.

He said very candidly that my presence had always reminded him of the tragic events involving my mother. One look at me and he would see my mother's face and relive the chaos of those early years of her insanity, my brother's death, and the confusion of what to do with me as a toddler while he worked long hours at Dedham Post Office.

He confided to me that his mode of dealing with me was pure and simple avoidance. In his own terms, I was an obstacle to the maintenance of peace in his troubled grieving mind. So he kept me at arm's length. Yet he apologized to me later for his self-centered neglect.

As for my own peace of mind, that was missing during much of my life. Abandonments and losses became a way of life for me. So true peace of mind was elusive, not just during my childhood but in later years.

Due to my experiences, I developed a tendency to distrust the possibility of having meaningful and stable relationships. Although I tried to achieve and maintain intimate long term relationships, in my heart lurked a dark message that those I depended upon would let me down sooner or later.

It is certainly a personal truth that based on my experiences in life I had deep seated trust issues. But from a spiritual perspective, didn't Jesus have trust issues too?

Jesus was betrayed repeatedly by those closest to him. They let him down and even lied about him under pressure. But he loved them despite their human flaws.

I think it was natural for him to be disappointed when betrayed by people he trusted. If so, why shouldn't I suffer that way too? Why should I expect a free ride in my life with everything going my own way? This is the kind of inner dialogue I have often had with myself.

Actually, I was not too surprised by my father's latest escapist behavior when I was not even finished high school. He had often abandoned me during my early years and eventually put me in a Catholic Charities home to preserve his own peace of mind.

Now the escape artist had to release himself from his secure job at the Dedham Post Office and escape to Maine to begin another more adventurous life.

As I look back at my own life in an effort to understand it better, I see how I played the role of the orphaned outsider, the misfit in society. I could see similarities and differences between my father's life and my own.

What was I escaping from? For the most part, I now believe I was escaping from memories of the trauma that I had suffered since early infancy and perhaps in the womb itself. I was told by my father that my arrival into life was the result of an "extremely difficult birth." So, in my case, life itself could be equated with trauma.

My early traumatic memories had no words connected with them. They were based on feelings I could not decipher and translate into words. The word "primal" might help explain the wounds that I carried since the birth process.

Doesn't everybody suffer this way? Not necessarily. PTSD following unthinkable pain cannot be accurately measured, as far as I know. It's an individual matter. And it is very complicated to analyze.

Even if two people suffer from very similar injuries there are differences in how they relate to the trauma, how they are affected, and how they react to their ensuing physical, mental, emotional, social and spiritual pain.

I will give you an example of how three people who have

experienced the same trauma may have extremely different memories of the situation.

Many years after leaving Mrs. White's house I had the opportunity to spend some time with two of the other boys who shared that Catholic Charities experience with me. We were together at that house in Norwood for six of the nine years I was there. And we were very close in age.

Decades after leaving Mrs. White's house, we were probably in our late thirties when I saw each of them on separate occasions. As we shared our tales of life with Mrs. White as our guardian, one of the men said to me calmly, "It wasn't so bad there." Most of his memories were positive.

When I saw the other man a year or so later I talked with him and his wife about our early years together with Mrs. White. She took me aside and whispered to me, "That woman ruined my husband's life."

Then I chatted with her husband alone for a while as we strolled around the property of the house we were visiting. We talked about our work histories, our families, and life itself. Among other things, I told him that Mrs. White had died when I was about to attend Boston College.

Without hesitation, he expressed in very angry terms the hate he had always felt for Mrs. White. The moment we began to discuss that part of our lives his anger seemed to be on the verge of rage.

In vivid earthy language, he told me that he still hated the very thought of her and he said to me, "If I could find her grave, I would go there and piss on it."

In my case, at that time in my life when I reflected back on my years in Norwood I had a middle of the road response. I indicated to each of the other men who had shared my time at Mrs. White's that there might have been a balance of good events along with many painful episodes.

So the three of us each had a different perspective on our

years with Mrs. White although many of our experiences at 42 Mountain Avenue had been identical or quite similar. One person thought he had not suffered very much there. The other person believed living there was ongoing torture. And the third saw both good and bad in the experience.

Obviously, we each had different levels of PTSD to deal with. And different responses. As the years passed, there were times when I could see myself functioning as a traumatized escapist like my father. Now I freely admit here and now that I have always been an escapist.

I escaped into reading books. I escaped into films. I escaped into romance. I escaped into habits such as the pursuit of silence. I escaped into writing books. Obsessive compulsive escape was my solution for many problems.

Fortunately, my escapist ability to cope with and enjoy silence became an asset as a student in schools and colleges. Silence based on self-restraint certainly helped me to become an outstanding student in my senior year at Dedham High where I continued to maintain Honor Roll status.

Then I took the entrance exam for Boston College which had its own examination. One of the high points of my life in the spring of 1949 was getting BC's letter of acceptance.

I was moved emotionally by that acceptance. Tears of gratitude filled my eyes as I read the letter. They were tears of amazement and joy. After all, I was not accustomed to having dreams fulfilled. Quite the opposite. I was more accustomed to having my dreams shattered.

However, attendance at Boston College was a very special dream. I had hung onto that dream for a long time. I had nurtured that dream. And I was not about to part with it.

Recalling my emotional response to the letter from BC, I have to admit that I am subject to extremes of emotion. I know I have always had excessive passion and sadness living underneath my misleading calm exterior.

From my earliest years I have had clashing aspects of pessimism and optimism. When something good seemed about to happen in my life, I might get excited about that, yet say in the next breath, "I wonder what will screw this up."

Seldom did my cherished dreams arrive on a platter. Obviously, I could not rely on others to help me achieve my goals. So I had to fend for myself, or as Granny might say, "forage" for myself. So the hard way was usually my way.

My father, by various quirks of fate, was often around to initiate the hard way for me. This was a pattern that I could never fully accept. Yet I had to learn to tolerate his actions or lack of action. What choices did I have?

Sure enough, within weeks after I had received my acceptance letter from Boston College, my father came down from Maine, showed up at Walnut Place, and informed me that it would not be possible for me to begin my college education that fall. Emotionally, this came at me like what some people describe as "a sucker punch."

He said start-up expenses for construction of Brookland Motor Court in Wells, Maine had used up Fred and Hazel's amassed money, including the money Granny had set aside to help with my higher education. So there was no other choice for the lone wolf orphan but to defer his plan to start B.C. in the fall of '49.

It was not the first time the lone wolf had faced challenging obstacles. And it would certainly not be the last. But who said life was supposed to be easy?

I think inspirational writer Scott Peck was right on the mark when he started his book *The Road Less Traveled* with the following sentence: "Life is difficult."

I don't think Peck meant that every minute of life is difficult. Neither did Mark Twain equate his own slant on life with his quote: "Life is one damn thing after another." But in my life, the Twain quote was often appropriate.

As for me, I think there is no such thing as a free ride through life as a first class passenger. Sure, some folks have more pleasant journeys. Some are born with silver spoons in their mouths. Others are immersed in misery. Most of us have ups and down. And nobody escapes challenges.

It's the times of crisis that make a meaningful life so interesting. And if some folks have more challenges than others, it's all part of their journey.

When I lived with my dramatic grandmother at 22 Walnut Place in East Dedham she would often make this comment about life: "'Tis no picnic. It's a vale of tears." Then she would tell stories about life in Ireland on the family farm in County Kerry before she came to the U.S. in her late teens.

Granny's stories did not have to be exaggerated. Her life in Ireland began while the British were still controlling Ireland and were organizing every aspect of an Irishman's life including the training of school teachers. The British gallows were still in the public squares.

She passed on to me some of the stories that her parents had told her about the terrible famine of the 1840s and 1850s. The famine drastically shrunk the population of the Irish nation through scarcity of food and widespread disease.

Workhouses and poorhouses existed throughout the starving nation. British landlords used Irish tenant farmers to plant crops that were harvested and then shipped from Irish harbors to England to feed that nation while Ireland starved.

Usually, I thought she was exaggerating, especially about the "vale of tears." But later in life there were times when my eyes would tear up as I nodded my head in the midst of a shocking setback or a daunting major challenge.

I would say in an Irish accent, "You were right, Granny. Praise be to God. 'Tis no picnic." Then I might say, "'Tis a conundrum, it is."

Chapter 7
Sojourn in Maine & Factory Education

When I graduated from Dedham High School with the class of '49 I was invited by my father to spend the summer with him and Hazel during the opening season of Brookland Motor Court on Route One in Wells, Maine. I accepted.

Part of the arrangement was that I would work a few hours daily with my father. The rest of my time would be my own. He was about to assemble two more cottages to expand the new complex to a dozen units. I was to be his helper.

Physically and emotionally, it was not the best summer I had ever spent. The space for the three occupants of "the office" was cramped. The small building served as a home for Fred and Hazel as well as the office for the field of housekeeping cottages.

It was the first time in my life that I functioned so closely with my father who was definitely not my choice for a house mate and work partner. As I have already noted more than a couple of times, there was a very high and impenetrable psychological wall between us.

Usually, through the sophomore and much of the junior year of high school when he was living with me at 22 Walnut Place, I did my best to keep myself remote from him in both mind and body. I operated like an invisible person, busy with my own activities and not curious about his.

As noted, it was self-defense. I was emotionally vulnerable around him. Painfully so. At Walnut Place under ordinary circumstances I could shrug off the negative energy that he stirred up in me. However, in Maine an air of diffidence was difficult to accomplish in close confinement.

We were so different temperamentally. He seemed to thrive on hard physical work. I was the opposite. I thrived on reading books. He moved his body with determination. I moved very slowly. He was muscular and strong. I had a painfully thin fragile body.

As usual, the summer heat drained my energy. He just shrugged off the heat. So we did not make a good construction team. But I could carry lumber, hold a ladder when he climbed, pass rafters and 2x4s to him, and bang nails to help with rough framing.

My psyche remained as conflicted about him as it had always been. In addition, my internal conflict was intensified because I was actually helping the parent who had sidetracked my plan to attend Boston College that fall.

It was an ongoing emotional conflict to work with him on the project that had become an obstacle to the fulfillment of my own educational destiny. Nevertheless, I tried to make a vacation out of that summer since I only worked a couple of hours each day with my father and had lots of free time.

So I would leave the motor court for a few hours, walk the mile-long Drakes Island Road to the beach, or hang out at the store there. However, for a shy person like me to be alone in a summer resort brought psychic discomfort.

In Maine my tendency toward loneliness intensified. Even though I have some strong lone wolf tendencies I have never been a recluse. I am comfortable being alone when I am reading or writing. But I need companionship.

I did not enjoy being away from my pals Fran, Mike and John who were back in Dedham, Massachusetts. At every phase in my life I have always needed good friends like my three pals and I have appreciated their friendship.

Even if I had a protective layer of "reserve" around my personality, that does not mean I was a total loner. So I anxiously looked forward to the end of a summer I did not consider to be a summer of good luck.

One bad omen took place at the beginning of the season.

The high school graduating class of '49 gold ring that I had worked and saved for had freed itself from my ring finger when a rogue wave hit me. Then the ring left with the tide.

As for my father, I simply did not enjoy his company. I was always edgy around him, living with a state of high alertness. The deep wounds he had left on my spirit were inoperable. So living in his shadow on a daily basis was an ongoing psychological endurance test for me.

One positive thing that summer of '49 was when Hazel's brother took me out on Route One and other Maine roads in his old 1934 Plymouth. He prepared me for my driver's license exam later that summer in Massachusetts.

There was a catch though. Russell had lost his own driver's license for a major infraction of the rules. He had earned an "indefinite" suspension that would probably keep him from regaining the driving privilege for many years. However, this did not deter Russell from teaching me.

He was unlicensed and Brookland Motor Court was directly opposite the Maine State Police barracks on Route One in Wells. But the daily training was performed. Luckily, Russell did not get caught giving me illegal driver training.

Actually, with me being an unlicensed driver at the wheel and my instructor having no license we were both lawbreakers. We could be viewed as "scofflaws" and I could have lost any eligibility for a license to drive.

By the end of summer in1949 I not only had my operator's license, Russell had turned his 1934 Plymouth coupe over to me. When summer was over, I made my first solo long distance journey. I drove my Plymouth along Route One through Maine, New Hampshire and Massachusetts and parked it in front of Granny's duplex.

At age 17 with my driver's license and my own car, I was a bit proud of those achievements. Then came the search for employment where I could save enough money in a year to enable me to finance my postponed first year at Boston College starting a year later in September 1950.

There was little work available in Dedham due to its lack of industry. But I landed a job locally at Boston Envelope Company. It was the first time I had punched a time clock at the beginning and end of a day of work.

The hourly rate as "floor boy" was 90 cents per hour. That pay would help me to save for my first year of BC. Also, Granny O'Connell allowed me to stay at her place without paying for room and board, so she subsidized my higher education. To this day I remain grateful for her assistance.

My envelope factory job is described in detail in my memoir *The O'Connell Boy: Educating the Wolf Child.* The main thing is that the factory work was steady and reliable. It was secure work because the world needed a daily supply of a wide variety of envelopes. And a floor boy was needed to haul thousands of envelopes to and from the machines each day and keep the glue pots filled. I was the floor boy.

With steady work I could count on the weekly paycheck and make regular deposits in my savings account at Dedham Institution for Savings. As the weeks and months passed and the savings grew, my own confidence about my future attendance at Boston College grew.

The idea of going to college was not just a wild fantasy. My work at the factory was going to make college a reality. Becoming a BC student was my most important goal. And I was determined to achieve that goal.

Keeping the old car going was a problem though. I had to go to the "Auto Save Yard" in the Readville section of Boston to scout for other 1934 Plymouths that might be rusting away in the auto grave yard.

I would remove the used parts and bring them to Leo Lore whose auto repair shop was on Curve Street in Dedham at the corner of Belknap Street opposite my grandfather's house. Then Leo would complain about the age of the Plymouth and its challenges. But he always got the job done with the used parts I delivered. His labor charge was small.

The condensed version of my '49 to '50 transition year is that I was in a state of limbo between high school and college. Also, I had deep anxiety about my college plans because of my father's unreliability. After all, life had shown me that the future was always predictably unpredictable.

In fact, the general idea among the Irish immigrant population where I had lived in Norwood was that one should avoid counting on positive outcomes. If a guy did that as he worked toward a cherished goal he was tempting fate.

One learned neither to assume nor brag. Also, it was not wise to voluntarily drop out of the industrial system. During the First Great Depression, jobs were very hard to come by

Up and down Washington Street, the main street in Norwood, and on side streets, stores went out of business. I have not seen that happen again until recent years during what I call the Second Great Depression. Now I see empty stores everywhere during this alleged "recovery."

Actually, in the late 1930s and early 1940s it did not take a genius to figure out that one's livelihood could move from an illusion of stability to total disaster in a few days. Strikes and layoffs were common. Also, one's plans could be set aside on short notice by the military draft in World War II.

I remember the negative impact of the Bird & Son plant shutdowns in nearby Walpole where many Norwood people were employed. Long gaps in employment could soon put a whole family on the brink of starvation. There wasn't much of a "safety net" provided by government or industry.

I recall that some factories in Norwood and vicinity habitually laid off workers just before the Christmas Season. Insecurity was a way of life if you were in the working class.

Did I say "class"? We usually didn't call ourselves

members of a class. In those days few people thought in terms of a defined class structure. We knew there was such a thing as extreme poverty and extreme wealth but most of us avoided placing ourselves in a category.

We were the land of opportunity, right? Our status was pretty much based on where we worked, where we lived, what kind of house sheltered us, or if we were in one of the rare families with a car. There was no car at Mrs. White's.

Income was a very private matter. As for housing, 42 Mountain Avenue in Norwood might not rank at the top of the status list nor did it rank low. It was a fine neighborhood with a variety of well maintained houses. Mrs. White's was among the largest. And her perfectionism kept it in immaculate condition. It was a "lace curtain Irish" house.

However, Granny's ancient duplex in East Dedham was in the blighted section of town. It would have been low on any status list. Yet Walnut Place, a "private way," was better than some other neighborhoods in East Dedham which had down-and-out Dickensian locations. I loved Walnut Place.

Regardless of where a person lived, basic security was greatly affected by job status. For people who had lived through the First Great Depression that I was born into in 1932, the word "security" was a key word in their lives.

As a result of their insecurity, people sought security in local, state and federal civil service jobs. The federal government's Postal Service ranked high in people's minds. Also, local police and fire departments, and the public schools, were all prized for the job security they offered.

Job security in those years about a decade after the depths of the First Great Depression made all the difference in a family's life. But because of my father's departure from the U.S. Post Office there would be no basic financial security in my own family life. Unpredictability would reign supreme.

Chapter 8
Boston College

In the fall of 1950, after working full-time for a year at the Boston Envelope Company's factory in Dedham, I started my freshman year at Boston College. It was a shaky beginning because of the financial situation.

I had worked and saved in a responsible way, but my father complicated the fiscal flow of my journey toward college. I had made the mistake of letting him know how much I was saving. And he could be very persuasive when he had a goal to achieve. Especially when it involved money.

In the spring of 1950 he had suddenly come down from Maine to 22 Walnut Place and requested a substantial loan from the funds he knew I had set aside for my use in college starting in the fall. At that point I had saved enough for tuition and books to get me through my entire freshman year.

For a change, I was beginning to feel secure. Then my father made his plea for funds with the promise that he would pay me back in the fall. I didn't trust his promise but I didn't know how to say no about the loan.

I made the serious error of lending him the lion's share of my college savings based on his promise to repay me in the fall after the fledgling motor court had amassed its first summer's earnings. The only wise thing I did at that time was to keep enough money in the bank to get me started with my first semester at BC.

In some ways Fred and I were accomplices in the restructuring of his new approach to life as an entrepreneur. He was my father, right? And even though he had some character deficits that impacted me severely, he was still my father and I believed he deserved any help I could give him.

Shortly after he had moved to Maine he asked me to be

silent about his location. He said the Commonwealth of Massachusetts was chasing him to obtain reimbursement for the long years of my mother's stay in State insane asylums.

I agreed to cover for him and sure enough, one day a State official knocked at Granny's door when I happened to be home. I was asked where my father was and I simply shrugged and said, "I don't know."

"Do you mean to tell me you actually don't know where your own father is located?"

"That's right. I don't know where my father is. I live here with my grandmother. My father doesn't live here."

"And you have no idea where he might be?"

"Right. I have no idea where he might be."

While this dialogue was going on I kept thinking of what a jerk the guy was. The more questions he asked me the more I disliked him. After all, I had always hated personal questions. And here was a guy who was getting paid for hounding people with his personal questions.

I'm surprised I didn't sarcastically ask, "Would you like to know what I had for breakfast?" But I restrained myself.

At any rate, I was not about to tell the guy what he wanted to know. And I was an expert at keeping secrets. I have never enjoyed lying but on some occasions I have been driven to it. This was one of those occasions. I had absolutely no guilt about what I was doing.

At the other end of the line in Maine, my father methodically placed the land and cottages of Brookland Motor Court in Hazel's name. The Commonwealth of Massachusetts was not going get its grasping hands on Hazel and Fred's livelihood. Not with Fred directing the evasion strategy. He was an expert at evasion.

At age 18, in September 1950 after a year of factory labor, I became a full-time student at Boston College. Those were the days when most B.C. students commuted to the campus. So that's what I did in the '34 Plymouth coupe. To keep the car going and fund my higher education adventure I needed to work at entry level part-time jobs.

Also, even though I hated the idea of hounding my absentee father, it was important for Fred to repay the money he owed me. He led me a merry chase because he was as adept at avoidance as I was at persistence. So I was forced to act like an earnest bill collector to get portions of the loaned money back into my depleted savings account.

It was about as pleasant a task as climbing a long hill in a sand and gravel pit. He repaid me very slowly. It took years of hounding to get him to fork over what he owed me. Semester after semester I teetered on the edge of a fiscal cliff. And this became an ongoing emotional drain.

Since birth my foremost emotion had been anxiety. Now the ongoing fiscal suspense during my college years was one more burden of heavy stress to carry. But what other choice did I have? I was determined to stick with college.

In those days few students at B.C. lived in dormitories. So I didn't have to cope with that expense. But the expense of being a commuter was a major challenge in its own right.

There was nobody to turn to for a loan of any kind. So it was one part-time job after another. Selling magazines. Baby sitting. Short order cook. Carpentry in the summer.

I pursued my Liberal Arts education with determination because it was the only kind of higher education that made sense to me. I was going to college to improve my mind, not to learn a trade. Nor was I there to pursue the opposite sex.

The student body at BC in those days was all male. The campus had an "old world" European Gothic flavor. But one day a week, nursing students and others came from BC's inner city satellite in Boston to take science and education courses on the main campus at Chestnut Hill.

I kept my distance from the women. That was easy to do

since I usually headed back to Dedham right after attending classes and studying at the Bapst Library. Also, warnings about women given to me by Mrs. White were imbedded deep in my psyche. And I had no money for dating.

As I began my Boston College education I was aware that many freshmen had attended BC High and a wide variety of private prep schools. They had an easy transition into higher education at BC. But after graduating from Dedham High School I too was well prepared for college. Without delay I became a Dean's List student.

Those of us who followed a classical education at BC in the College of Arts and Sciences had a structured curriculum. As entering freshmen we had a choice of two paths to follow for two years: A.B. Greek or A.B. Math.

I chose Math. This means that along with courses in Latin, French, History, Literature and Science we also had to deal with advanced courses in Math which was not my favorite subject. But I stayed on the Dean's List.

We also had a heavy dose of Theology as a required subject regardless of one's major field of study. Later we had a very heavy dose of required courses in Philosophy. I believe I had more courses in Philosophy than in my major. But for me, studying philosophy was a labor of love and healthy exercise for my inquiring mind.

As I approached my junior year I chose History & Government as my major field of study. I chose this because I was inspired by Professor Thomas O'Connor who was just starting his career as a professor and had almost the same name as mine except for a couple of letters in his last name.

I had experienced him in a required History course and it was a pleasure to be one of his students. This true gentleman was an outstanding scholar with a relaxed and very knowledgeable manner. He made history interesting and worth pursuing.

Our professors during my time at BC were a mix of Jesuit priests and laymen. From my perspective, they were the cream of the crop. The education I received at BC proved to be an ideal foundation for a life of ongoing learning in various fields of endeavor as well as spiritual development.

Harvard not only held no interest for me; I made wisecracks about the place. "You can always tell a Harvard man but you can't tell him much." "A typical Harvard man would flunk out of Boston College in the first semester."

I worked my way through the first three years of college going full-time days while being employed part-time in factories and other odd jobs. Summers I worked full-time on construction as a carpenter building houses in suburbs west of Boston including Waltham, Needham and Medfield.

As I reflect on the years I spent pursuing my higher education, I also think of Granny O'Connell's comment: "Ye're burning the candle at both ends, Tommy."

Granny was right. It was an intense cycle of college studies, part-time jobs, and drinking beer with my pals while trying to abide by the slogan "All work and no play makes Tom a dull boy."

It caught up to me as I entered my junior year of college. That summer had been a period of long hours at carpentry work and very heavy drinking with my pals. Adding to my individual stress was the challenge of maintaining the old car and paying my tuition for the coming year.

Also, in the realm of fulfilling a fantasy the four of us pals chipped in for a piece of land at Rexhame Shores in Marshfield, Massachusetts. There we tried to erect a summer cottage for ourselves a short distance from the ocean.

That project was our idea of paradise on Earth. We were building our own place to invite girls and live the carefree young bachelor life. However, the cottage that was going to feed our sensual imaginations didn't get completed.

Mike went into the Air Force, John into the Army, Fran into the Navy. I had my draft deferment as long as I would remain in college. The rough frame for the dream cottage was boarded in and would stand there in all kinds of weather for many years to come with its complicated hip roof and windows completed, the rest only partially finished.

That "old gang of mine" was breaking up. So the cottage was put on hold. Also, I had fallen in love. And as I burned the candle at both ends, I was beginning to get an array of frightening physical symptoms.

I had truly gone beyond my personal limits of endurance. Now, as Granny O'Connell would predict, I was about to "pay the piper." In some ways it's easy to look back and see what was happening to me. But living with the challenges was another matter. My symptoms took on a life of their own, impairing me psychologically as well as physically.

As a result, I was living in a state of ongoing terror, wondering if I might be on the verge of a catastrophic illness that would kill me. I am not exaggerating. I was having panic attacks and did not know until decades later what a panic attack truly consisted of. They are very frightening.

My balance was off and I had frequent dizzy spells. I had vertigo. I had asthmatic breathing difficulties. My blood pressure rose to dangerously high levels. My heart raced far beyond the normal pulse rate of 70 as tachycardia pushed it to 140 so often that it became a chronic condition. I also had chronic digestive problems and was in a state of constant fatigue and weakness.

Paradoxically, when some U.S. Marine Corps recruiters came to the B.C. campus I applied for their ROTC program and reached the point of taking the physical. But I flunked the physical because of the racing pulse and what they called an "anxiety state." For me, anxiety was a steady state.

Chapter 9
Marriage, Army & Back to College

I was in a state of exhaustion so deep and oppressive that as I look back now it is hard to find the words to express how I felt on a daily basis. Actually, I felt as if I were about to completely collapse and die. This is no exaggeration.

Using earthy language I would describe the situation this way: "My ass was really dragging." I felt as if I would just as soon lie down on the ground or on the floor and stay there.

But I have always had a strong will. So I trudged along through the fatiguing wilderness that comprised much of my emotional life. My brain and the part that is described as my body have always been out of sync. I live mostly in my head.

I could not share my challenging reality with anybody. I just functioned, that's all, as I plodded through steps leading to goals and from one goal to another.

No matter how convoluted my thinking might be, I always thought of myself as a logical person with a very intelligent mind. As a friend of mine wisecracked, "Tom is a legend in his own mind." Tom, the mastermind.

The mastermind's plan unfolded in the year 1953. The plan: At the end of junior year at BC I would drop college for a time and notify the local Draft Board. They would discontinue my deferment and put me on the list to enter compulsory military service.

I would marry and find a temporary residence. We would live there until the Draft Board inducted me into the U.S. Army. Then my partner would move in with her parents while waiting to join me wherever the Army assigned me.

I would serve my two years in the Army and qualify for the G.I. Bill which would later help subsidize my senior year of college. I would strive to graduate with honors and would live happily ever after as I pursued my chosen career.

Does this sound like a pipedream? For me, my master plan was a logical plan. In the meantime, while living in Dedham I worked at Dowding Tap Company a few miles away in Norwood. I was assigned to the shipping room until I was laid off. It was not a good time to be unemployed.

But I stuck to my master plan. You might say I activated the plan by getting married in November 1953 when I was in a fundamental state of poverty. Money? Who needs money? Love conquers all, right?

Then I arranged for a brief honeymoon in a large new motel near the rotary circle in Portsmouth, New Hampshire. After that came several days during the tourist off-season at my father's Brookland Motor Court in Wells, Maine.

Back home in Dedham I found work with the Zoppo Construction Company in Norwood as time keeper on their College Town Sportswear building. This moderately sized building was being constructed on Morrissey Boulevard in Dorchester near the *Boston Globe* and across the street from the new massive Columbia Point public housing project.

For our own housing, I located a small apartment on Belknap Street at Curve Street in East Dedham across the street from Leo Lore's Auto Repair Shop.

The apartment was in the decaying 12- room house that had once provided the domicile for Grandpa Dan O'Connell and Granny Johanna and their five children, comprised of three sons and two daughters.

When I moved in, the house at Belknap Street was owned jointly by my Uncles Joe and Bill. They had restructured it into four apartments after ownership was conveyed to them.

This location would be home until my Army induction. At that time my spouse would move back in with her parents who were relocating from Norwood into their new home in Franklin. That would be my home address during my early months of Army service. In the meantime I would continue to work as time keeper on the College Town Sportswear building in Dorchester.

As already noted, I thought the plan I had devised was intelligent. After all, wasn't I a very logical person? And hadn't countless thousands of other guys experienced military life and fared well?

Also, the combat of the Korean Conflict had ended in 1953. Why shouldn't I do fine in the Army of 1954? The answer is that I was unprepared for the psychological harassment the U.S. Army inflicts on new recruits.

Adding to the adjustment challenge, I was married and expecting my first child. Also, I was 22 and accustomed to making my own decisions. Did I say something about decisions? My life was about to change dramatically, especially when it came to making decisions.

Once again, as could happen when the impulsive part of my nature dominated, I was in denial about the realities of the life of an Army private. The Army would make all decisions and I would have no right of dissent.

Since leaving Mrs. White's house I had developed a powerful resistance to any and all authority figures who thought they could boss me around. Therefore, I rapidly learned that Army life was alien to my very being.

To say it in a few well chosen words, I was just not cut out for two years of Army life. It was one of the most horrendous experiences of my life. It was mental torture. And I had entered into it voluntarily. So it was self-torture.

NOTE: This brings me to the point where my U.S. Army memoir began on March 15, 1954. That story about my two years as a military misfit is called *Bugging Out: An Army Memoir (1954)*. My Sanctuary Book is available through Amazon.com and Barnes & Noble bookstores.

Back to my story. Through a process that must have

involved divine intervention I managed to rise through the enlisted ranks from private to specialist third class. Miraculously, I avoided court martials and instead was recommended for the Good Conduct Medal.

When I completed my two "active duty" Army years, I received the National Defense Service Medal, plus a "Special Commendation" for the "outstanding service" I had performed at the Provost Marshal General's School (PMGS) in my role as public information specialist.

In those days, men had to serve eight years in the military to complete their obligation. This included two years of full-time service plus six years in the Army Reserve. Then would come the receipt of the long awaited Honorable Discharge.

During the six years in the inactive reserve in the Eisenhower years there was the ongoing anxiety that an international incident would put me in a category in which I could be recalled to the nightmare of serving on active duty. I was grateful this did not happen. Although Ike had been a military leader, as President he astutely avoided war.

Actually, the Army provided some training that was useful later in civilian life. I learned to touch type while with the Army's only Military Government (MG) Group at Camp Gordon, Georgia. Also, I gained experience as feature editor of our MG newspaper. And at PMGS I gained expertise in writing many feature stories for magazines and newspapers.

Back in civilian life, I followed my logical master plan. Using the G.I. Bill, I entered my senior year at Boston College. I worked in a factory full-time nights and attended B.C. full-time days. Soon I found my family an apartment in the Dedham Veterans Housing project at East Dedham.

I completed my Bachelor of Arts Degree in History & Government *cum laude* in 1957.

Chapter 10
Work (Amica Insurance) and Family

Through the balance of the Eisenhower 1950s and onward, family life continued. In 1954 while I was in the Army, our first child Peggy was born. Next, in 1957, came our middle daughter Karen. In 1961 our third daughter Amy emerged. Also, that year I was awarded my Master of Arts Degree in History from Boston U. Nine years after Amy, in 1970, our son Sean arrived.

Four seemed to be the ideal number of children, although population control fanatics might think otherwise. Each of my children is precious and they have made our world a better place. This is also true of nine grandchildren and the current six great grandchildren. My family is still growing.

My very recent 2013 memoir, *Upward & Downward Mobility: A Work Memoir*, gives a detailed overview of the varied assortment of jobs I held during my working years.

For the most part, work for me has always been an important segment of my life. But seldom did I share work stories with my family or friends. I simply did my work and avoided talking about it when I was home or with friends.

I can find no better commentary on my relationship with the world of work than a few well chosen words in a prayer written by the philosopher and genius Sir Francis Bacon (1561-1626):

He thanks the Lord for "the gracious talent of your gifts and graces." Then he says he "misspent it in things for which I was least fit; so I may truly say, my soul has been a stranger in the course of my Pilgrimage."

My soul was also a stranger during my pilgrimage through occupations that provided the income to support my growing family over the years. Eventually, I was able to nurture my soul better by avoiding "leadership" positions.

I am not saying that my work life was useless. In fact, many of the goals I achieved in my varied occupations helped humanity and were worthy of respect.

However, working for wages as a leader or as an employee was not my cup of tea. There were drawbacks to functioning in leadership or staff positions.

Acting as a "front man" for nonprofit organizations, I was useful to the groups that hired me for my executive abilities. But no matter how worthy the cause, my soul did not feel fulfilled by my activities as an executive.

I think the work that best suited my freelance personality was my several years (1957-1961) as an accident claims investigator for AMICA Insurance Company.

In my first position after graduating from Boston College I was a specialist, not a leader or a follower. That suited me. It was interesting work and provided a company car along with the freedom of scheduling my own time. I performed my investigations in the Greater Boston area and later did similar work in New Hampshire and Maine.

But I was itching to find work that involved writing. This led me into administrative work with health and human service organizations as well as trade associations. My work put me into staff and Chief Executive roles with four different organizations in the fields of accident prevention, the auto industry, public housing, and long term healthcare.

My leadership positions were very educational for me and others. Also, they provided me with a middle class lifestyle, prestige, and high visibility in the mass media.

However, for a fundamental introvert and an orphan, the intensity of my work also put a strain on my sensitive nervous system. I was often in the situation that I found in a wonderful cartoon when I was very young. It reflected my mental state in the world of employment by others.

The cartoon depicted two college professors in their academic robes, and each one held a large book with a bold title on the cover. These were the titles: "What to do" and "Don't do it."

I had a talented artist create a similar cartoon for me recently. If you would like a copy of it , send your request to me at P.O. Box 25, Dennisport, MA 02639 and enclose five dollars for postage and handling.

In the nonprofit world, each position I held challenged my emotional balance on a regular basis. Why? Because the Chief Executive of a nonprofit organization is immersed in the world of committees.

In nonprofits it's all about committees. The board of directors that hires you is a committee. Then there is the executive committee of the board that works with you to meet the organization's goals. And there are a variety of committees to carry out the mission of the organization.

If you wish to look at the world we live in objectively, it's a world of committees. Whether in public or private sectors, I found a bewildering and exhausting world of committees and subcommittees. I experienced an infinity of committees.

I was so involved in committee work that eventually I was afflicted with a powerful allergy to committees of all kinds. You might say that I overdosed on committees.

People who overdose on strawberries often find themselves allergic to the berries they were addicted to. Eventually, I contracted a behavioral aversion to committees.

On the plus side, I was also getting to do some writing along the way. Newsletters. Annual reports. Radio and TV public service messages. News releases. Feature stories. You name it; I wrote it.

My goal had been to hold positions requiring some writing. So the world of nonprofits was the place that satisfied that need for me in those days.

Chapter 11
Mass. Safety Council & Chevy Dealers Assoc.

From age 30 to 32 I served as Public Information Director and Fund Raiser for the Massachusetts Safety Council, Inc. I honed my mass media writing skills there and overcame my extreme shyness as I developed the ability to serve as a professional public speaker representing the Council.

Also, I organized fund raising efforts. I can't say that I enjoyed the work but it was tied directly to my job survival. The goal of my first year with the Council was to raise enough funding to pay my salary as Public Information Director for the following year. I achieved the goal. Finally I had qualified for a job that primarily involved writing.

To satisfy a political ambition, at age 32 (1964) I won election to the Dedham School Committee, a nonsalaried public service post. I soon became Vice Chairman and Chairman. At age 34 I was featured in the *Dedham Transcript* as the youngest School Committee Chairman in the history of the colonial town founded in 1636.

Also, at age 32 I became Executive Director of the Chevrolet Dealers Association, Inc. serving dealers in Massachusetts and Rhode Island. My automotive experience with Amica Insurance and my association executive experience with the Safety Council helped me win that leadership position. I stayed there for five years, until 1968.

In my late 30s I began to concentrate on writing fiction while I was still running the Chevy Dealers organization and serving on the Dedham School Committee. This was also the period when I began to experience an irritable bowel, diabetes, depression, and increasing relationship problems.

At age 35 (1967), after re-evaluating my life, I resigned the chairmanship of the School Committee and decided to put my energy into my writing. At this time I bought a cottage near Perkins Cove next to the Museum of Modern Art of Ogunquit in Maine. I envisioned writing novels there.

A year later, at age 36, I resigned from the Dedham School Committee after being re-elected to a three year term and completing one year. Hoping a geographical change made sense, I moved with my family to Maine and lived year-round in the cottage where I completed my first novel.

As my fiction writing obsession grew, I produced my second and third novels. Now I had three novels but I still did not find approval by the publishers in New York.

During the period from 1968 to 1970, in my late '30s, I decided to leave the Chevrolet Dealers Association. The job market was difficult but I was able to return to insurance claims work with the Crum & Forster Companies, handling their Maine and New Hampshire claims from their branch office in Portland, Maine where I spent one day a week.

I continued writing fiction each day while investigating accidents. It seemed like an idyllic existence living on the Maine coast with my family. I survived economically and was able to use my creativity.

Writing more and more fiction, I attracted agent Howard Moorepark in New York but still had no success with the major publishers. This did not stop me from producing more fiction. I was driven by energies I cannot explain.

While in Maine I also experimented with teaching at the college level. I taught Philosophy and Logic for New Hampshire College. This experience proved to be useful many years later.

A special highlight of my Maine adventure was the birth of our fourth child, Sean Thomas O'Connell, in June 1970. He brought joy to me and my family then. And he still does.

Chapter 12
Boston Public Housing Tenants Policy Council (TPC)

I now look back on the three years in Maine as my "Great Gatsby Years." I am not exaggerating when I say that being in Ogunquit ("Beautiful Place by the Sea") and constantly writing essays and novels was living out a writer's fantasy.

Our location on Shore Road next to artist Henry Strater's Ogunquit Museum of Art was one of the most beautiful places in the world. Each year at his colorful opening and closing ceremonies we were invited guests.

A brief walk from our acreage next to the Museum led to Narrow Cove with its unusual pebble beach at the edge of the Atlantic Ocean. A few yards away was scenic Perkins Cove where I moored my Boston Whaler. This was a long way from the Catholic Charities home with Mrs. White and Granny's duplex next to the East Dedham Railroad Station.

I struggled to achieve some success with my writing. But the long winters in Maine became times that challenged my confidence in my own creativity. The world was apparently not waiting for my fiction. And I found this depressing.

It became obvious to me that the family would benefit from a return to Massachusetts where I was determined to engage in human services whether in health, welfare, or education. My goal was to be more useful to humanity.

The work situations I will describe very briefly here are discussed in depth in my recent book *Upward & Downward Mobility: A Work Memoir.*

The position that made the return to Dedham in 1971 possible was one of the most difficult jobs I had ever held. I plunged head first into Boston politics when I served as Executive Director of the Boston Public Housing Tenants Policy Council (TPC), a nonprofit agency that represented the 55,000 tenants who lived in Boston's numerous public housing projects.

In my role as Executive Director of the Tenants Policy Council, I reported to a large and unwieldy board of forty-two directors of varying ethnicity who represented the many public housing projects sprinkled throughout the city. When I was hired, the board did not inform me that the funding was about to run dry. The job only lasted several months.

The problems of Boston's projects were immense. The pressure I felt in my job was unbelievably intense. Looking back, I think it was beyond any person's ability to handle it.

Dealing with the Boston Housing Authority (BHA) and other political entities was educational but also exhausting. The orphan who worked better at a reasonable pace was not cut out for such a high pressure job.

The difficulties of resettling in Dedham were challenging too. We finally leased a house next to a church in the middle class Oakdale section of town.

In short order I had to line up a different job that would enable me to support my family. But before I left the TPC I put my energy into organizing a drive that was successful in achieving a new precedent-setting tenant's rights agreement with BHA, along with a grievance procedure for the tenants.

Also, just before departing, I arranged a highly publicized fact-finding tour of Boston's housing projects by U.S. Senator Edward Brooke. Then I left the TPC with the feeling that I had made a real contribution to the 55,000 tenants.

Was I useful as TPC Executive Director? Yes. Was I glad to move on because of the lack of funding? Yes. Was it a valuable experience even though the problems of Boston's public housing projects were mind boggling? Sure. All my experiences in life, no matter how challenging, have been valuable. I have learned much from each experience. And I consider myself lucky to have survived them all.

Chapter 13
Massachusetts Federation of Nursing Homes

I view the early '70s as an example of the old saying, "He jumped from the frying pan into the fire." My next job put me under indescribable stress for three years and tested my physical and mental endurance.

To win that job in 1972 I entered a competition with about 100 other applicants for the role of Executive Director of the Massachusetts Federation of Nursing Homes. It happened to be headquartered in my hometown of Dedham.

I won the contest, but three months later when the search committee's second choice visited me, I told him, "Jim, when you didn't get this job, you were very lucky. The intensity is beyond belief." That job gave me some of the most stressful and fatiguing years of my adult life, ranking along with my two years as a misfit in the U.S. Army.

From 1972 to 1975, as Executive Director of the trade association representing more than 300 nursing homes and other healthcare facilities in Massachusetts, one of my priorities was to expand government relations and win governmental agency reorganization at the state level.

I became a registered lobbyist at the State House, taking guidance from highly skilled professional lobbyists hired by the Federation. I succeeded in coordinating a dynamic campaign to persuade Governor Frank Sargent to enact a deficiency budget to pay some 70 million dollars in overdue obligations to health care providers in the Bay State. This was easier said than done because the Governor had made a pledge to file no deficiency budgets. But our coalition won.

However, I was once again pressing my luck with my health, and I began to feel deeply "burned out" physically and emotionally. The intensity of the job was extreme.

In a few words, the pressure of this CEO position was intolerable. I felt totally trapped. Jobs were scarce because we were in a recession. The pay was excellent with superb benefits. I was taking all-expense paid business trips to attend conferences in places like Hawaii and San Francisco. But that did not offset the problem of excessive stress.

Despite the fact that some good things were happening, I was overwhelmed by the high visibility life I was leading. I was thrust into State politics but constitutionally unsuited to play such a role. To express how I felt about my life, here is what I wrote to myself at that time: "My world looks bleak."

I have already mentioned Sir Francis Bacon and how he felt about the intense pressure of the life he was living. The sentiments offered in his prayer certainly applied to me in the 1970s. Surely my life seemed to me to be "misspent in things for which I was least fit; so I may truly say, my soul has been a stranger in the course of my pilgrimage."

It was obvious that I was not cut out for the pressure I had chosen to accept when I agreed to serve as CEO for the trade association representing the long-term healthcare facilities in Massachusetts. I was overwhelmed right from the first day. And the pressure never eased off.

I was haunted by exhaustion at work and in other aspects of my life. A skin cancer appeared behind my right ear. Blood pressure zoomed upward. My family doctor said I was experiencing "nervous exhaustion." My aorta was giving off ominous loud sounds. A beloved uncle was dying of cancer.

In January 1973 a virus infection struck me with a vengeance and left me feeling totally beat and very weak from the waist down to my toes. It was as if some switch in my energy system had clicked off. That loss of energy was destined to last for many more years. It was only will power and the Grace of God that kept me going from day to day.

So the word "bleak" continued to characterize the world I

was inhabiting. I was not simply depressed or dead tired and exhausted; I was feeling that no aspect of my life had a good outlook. I was wondering if I had ever made a healthy decision about any part of my life. And I was doubting whether I would ever be capable of healthy decisions.

My existence at that time became very shaky. On a daily basis I believe I was functioning very close to the dividing line between life and death. As I plodded along through life there were times when it did not seem that my feet were touching the ground when I walked. And there were other times when I felt weighted down like a deep sea diver.

The extreme loneliness that had always afflicted this orphan to some degree became almost unbearable. And because of the depths of the negative feelings about the stress, I often thought I must be on the verge of death.

Although I kept working on my novels and had outstanding literary agents from New York City and Beverly Hills representing me, my books were still unpublished.

In spite of the lavish nature of a truly fabulous junket to England, the years had taught me that various pleasures and successes in my life have always carried a steep price.

My body and psyche have been relatively unconcerned with success and instead have preferred a moderate pace, creative satisfaction, and balance. These factors were not available to me during the 1970s.

One stress after another built at this time and I was beginning to feel like the living embodiment of the mythological Sisyphus who was doomed to keep rolling a huge rock up a hill, only to have it roll back down, forcing him to keep pushing it back up again ...without end.

Suffering from chronic fatigue and sadness, I nevertheless organized great legislative victories and was a mass media personality. Also, I attracted the recognition of my peers, and served on boards of directors of professional societies.

However, there was something fundamentally wrong. I was quite successful in the eyes of the world, yet I felt trapped by my own life. My writing goals had not paid off except in minor ways. I felt I was not measuring up to my hopes and dreams. And this depressed me greatly.

Adversity proved helpful. In the midst of my suffering I discovered the work of psychologist Carl Jung. His work helped me in my own search for meaning in my life. I could relate to Jung's thinking, and I credit his work with getting me to see life from a more healthy perspective.

With the help of my Jungian studies, I began to look deeply into my own soul. Then it became obvious that I had to part company with the nursing home association and change the direction I was following.

I started looking for a college teaching job as a way to bail out after three years of exhausting intensity in the field of long term health care. I thought I might find a workplace "home" in the field of higher education, having experienced some of that more satisfying way of life while in Maine, teaching Logic and Philosophy at New Hampshire College.

But the entry pay level for new college professors was nowhere near what I needed to meet obligations. How did I feel? Like a man on a dead end street with no visible exit.

But right then, a friend said he had heard about the coming retirement of the current CEO of the Massachusetts Safety Council, where I was Public Information Director ten years earlier. It sounded like a perfect opportunity for me to pursue…with whatever guidance the Lord might provide. So I intensified my prayer life.

Chapter 14
CEO: Massachusetts Safety Council, Inc.

The screening process for the Safety Council job was almost over when I entered the competition. But I was confident, having been the Council's Public Information Director a decade earlier.

Now, in 1975, I was optimistic about returning to an important role in accident prevention. The Council had moved its offices from Devonshire Street to an ideal location on Beacon Street at the top of the Hill. The large suite of offices was up above Goodspeed's Book Shop, across from the long wide steps of the front entrance to the State House.

However, as I was about to take the elevator up to the higher level where the Mass. Safety Council's Executive Committee was going to interview me, an ominous event took place. I began to feel amazingly weak, with symptoms similar to the flu. I felt "a pit in my stomach" and weak legs. But I decided to ignore the feeling.

When the screening was finished a few weeks later I had the job, and feeling a bit like Rip Van Winkle, I went back to head up the organization I had left ten years before. Now, at age 43, my weary spirits began to lift.

As CEO of the Massachusetts Safety Council, Inc., once again I had the mission of preventing accidents on the highways, in the home, and the workplace. Shortly, although I took a large cut in salary to change jobs, I felt recharged with energy and set ambitious goals for the organization.

My private office was very large and through a huge bay window I had a spectacular view of the glistening golden dome of the State House. As I sat in a comfortable swivel chair with a leather seat I could spin between two desks.

One desk faced the bay window and the golden view. The

other desk had a massive conference table extending out from it so that we could hold small meetings there. And the table gave me plenty of space to spread out paper work.

I had the feeling that I had finally "arrived" at a place that suited my intelligence and creativity, not to mention my brain and my central nervous system.

To achieve the Council's goals, I attracted new funding from the auto insurance industry for media campaigns on the need to support the 55 mph speed limit. We started with the slogan "55 Will Get You There…Safer, Cheaper, Calmer." After a while we just said, "55 Will Get You There." My campaign attracted attention both regionally and nationally.

Much later, I launched a dynamic highway courtesy campaign that carried the slogan, "A Little Courtesy Won't Kill You." Due to the nature of my work, I became a highly visible spokesperson in the news and information media.

There was much satisfaction in the position I held. It seemed for a while to be the kind of place where I might stay for a long time, right into retirement. I might even be tempted to abandon my concept of five-year plans that kept me moving from job to job.

Around this time I was appointed to the Governor's Highway Safety Committee under Governor Mike Dukakis. Also, in Chicago I served on the Executive Committee of National Safety Council's Conference of State and Local Safety Organizations.

The boy from the other side of the tracks, in the shadow of the East Dedham railroad station, had come a long way. I had the family home in Dedham in the middle class Oakdale section of town. Also, I had the place on the Maine coast in Ogunquit next to the Ogunquit Museum of Modern Art, one of the most beautiful locations on the planet.

I was a highly visible figure in one of the nation's major metropolitan areas. And I was able to use my intelligence and creativity in useful ways to benefit the human race. So the world seemed to be my oyster. But there were other thoughts competing for space in my head.

Was this too good to be true? Or did it reflect the title of George Bernard Shaw's play *Too True To Be Good*?

Was I on wings with wax fasteners and flying too close to the sun as the mythological Icarus had done?

During my rise to the top had I forgotten about Granny O'Connell's favorite comment on success? "The closer you are to the top the closer you are to the door."

When I was at the height of my mass media visibility, the President of the *Boston Globe* Newspaper Company, John Giuggio, approached me at a meeting we were attending in the *Globe's* executive dining room.

Commenting on the widespread exposure I was receiving in the mass media, he asked seriously, "Tom, would you be interested in running for Governor?"

I knew in my heart that total involvement in politics would be disastrous for me. So my response required no deliberation. "No, John. Thanks for asking, but I've been over-exposed to politics. That way of life doesn't interest me." An even more candid expression of truth would have been that the political way of life nauseated me.

Also, I was in no physical or mental condition to even consider such a way of life. My exhausted feeling was constant. Intestinal problems arose. High blood pressure continued. Tears would come into my eyes for no apparent reason. Tranquilizers did not help. Alcohol was no solution because a depressant drug is not an antidote for exhaustion.

In those days, while some folks on my Board of Directors good naturedly called me Mr. Safety Council, behind the scenes I had some militant opposition to contend with, and it wore at my patience. I would win battle after battle but I got very tired of fighting the battles. Contention exhausted me.

One illustrious gentleman who was a high level volunteer at the Council adopted the role of "devil's advocate" when it came to any recommendation I would make at an Executive Committee meeting. He was not just an ant at my picnic; he was an irritating mosquito.

He tried to get me to back down from my own plan of action for the Council, but I refused. Then he threatened me with a statement indicating that I would live to regret my decision not to go along with him. I decided to ignore him.

For the rest of my time at the Safety Council he held on to his negativity toward me. His status in society was so high that people rarely got in his way as I was doing. So he was relentless in his enmity toward me.

Interestingly, we were both Catholics who made visits to the same Catholic chapel on the street leading to the State House. To this day, I believe we both prayed for the Lord to vanquish the opposition we were receiving from each other.

My adversary was an ongoing challenge for my status as a practicing Christian. I had to pray constantly for the grace to forgive him. And he gave me plenty of opportunities to pray for the grace I needed. He provided an endless string of challenges to my integrity and my endurance.

One day many years after I had left the Council I was in Boston on foot, crossing an intersection near Beacon Street. I saw an old blind man with a white cane waiting to cross. Then I realized it was my former adversary. I was tempted to keep walking.

Then I recalled Jesus' counsel that we should love our enemies, so I decided to introduce myself. After having a brief chat with him about our times at the Safety Council I helped him get safely across the street.

As we parted, he thanked me and we shook hands. That chance meeting seemed to bring a kind of spiritual closure to a very uncomfortable episode in my life.

Although there was much satisfaction to be gained at the Safety Council, administration of any kind had always gone against my grain. Hiring and firing personnel, and needing to supervise them, was definitely not my cup of tea.

Also, it was a debilitating energy drain to deal with adversaries who had nothing better to think about than undermining my efforts on behalf of the Council.

Actually, as I look back objectively to my years of serving as CEO of four nonprofit organizations, I believe I was in the advanced stages of career burnout. I had no tolerance left for the kind of employment I had chosen.

Four leadership positions had taught me that the person at the top is not only a target, but actually a bull's-eye at the heart of the target.

Therefore, in 1978 after much reflection and having had a spiritual awakening, I decided to leave the Massachusetts Safety Council. My key volunteer, President Peter Quinn, and others at the Council tried to talk me into staying but I felt I had to set myself free to move on with my life.

Each year the arrival of June 14 always reminds me of my beloved Uncle Joe's death early in June of '78. It also reminds me of the day I was given a goodbye celebration by the leaders of the Safety Council.

Board President Peter Quinn presided over the gathering of the Board of Directors at the Massachusetts Safety Council's Annual Meeting. He presented the Certificate of Appreciation to me at the impressive Pier Four restaurant on the Boston waterfront for my "efforts to prevent death and injury resulting from accidents."

At age 46, that turned out to be my last day of full-time employment. "Free at last!" The day was Flag Day, June 14, 1978, the beginning of a new stage in my life. The next stage would be very productive and would expand my personal freedom and creativity.

Chapter 15
Freelance Communications Consultant

Soon after leaving the Council when I had been at the height of success in accident prevention and Boston area fame, I rapidly plummeted into a deep valley of financial distress. And I was speedily removed from my status as a constantly visible media personality. "Tom Who?"

As I look back at my personal history, it is obvious that God had other plans than the ones I had devised for myself. I had hoped to set up my own nonprofit organization but I could not attract the funding no matter how hard I tried.

I doggedly persisted with the attempt into late 1978, until all of my financial resources had dried up and my mortgage on the house in Dedham was in serious jeopardy.

To get from week to week, I signed on with a temp agency that handled organizations in the Route 128 industrial area near Boston and soon I was earning what I describe as survival pay at rates near the bottom of the income ladder.

Then, in a burst of what I considered to be divine intervention, my public communication expertise led to an unsolicited invitation to serve a division of Tufts/New England Medical Center in Boston. This was additional confirmation of the tea bag label that had once informed me, "Life is what happens while you are making other plans."

It was also a time when I deepened my walk with God by studying to become a Secular Franciscan, meaning I was trying to be one who is "in the world but not of the world." I have been a Catholic Christian Franciscan ever since.

The project for Tufts had led me into a reluctant decision to become a communications consultant to health and human service organizations as a way of life. With Tufts as my first freelance client, I began soliciting additional work.

Within six months I had as many clients as I could handle, was earning as much as I had received at the Safety Council, and had the freedom of managing my own affairs instead of coping with a board of directors.

Since parting company with the Mass. Safety Council, I have never worked a full-time schedule as an employee. In other words, as Clark Gable commented on "working for wages" in his last film "The Misfits" (1961), I have not worked for full-time "wages" since Flag Day, June 14, 1978.

Instead, as Gable's character in the film had chosen to do, I became a confirmed freelance misfit. Freedom has always been more important to me than financial security and workplace conformity. It has not been an easy road to follow through the wilderness of dependence on good will and paid invoices by clients. But it has been worth it.

Some people live in tents in the woods to avoid workplace slavery. They see a steady salary as a hindrance, not a benefit. In some ways, I am a lot like those people.

Now, as a freelance, I was embarked on a journey based on my own skills and talents. My expertise as a mass media campaigner, freelance writer, and editorial consultant led me to assignments with many United Way organizations and other health and human services enterprises.

During the late 1970s and up to the 1990s I worked with clients such as hospitals, visiting nurse associations, addiction treatment centers, educational entities, lung associations, and family service agencies.

For several years I served as communications consultant for the American Lung Association of Massachusetts and other local lung associations of the Greater Boston area.

Among a host of other public communication activities, I had the responsibility for organizing the annual Christmas Seal Campaign kickoff at the Sheraton Boston Hotel.

At the American Lung Association office in Boston near

the waterfront I was provided with a desk, part-time secretarial assistance, and an arrangement where I spent a full day in their offices once a week. It was one of the finest media consulting experiences of my freelance career.

One of my most interesting smoking cessation awareness projects at the Lung Association was working with *Boston Globe* cartoonist Paul Szep who had been the recipient of Pulitzers. He became our honorary Christmas Seal Campaign Chairman and filled that role with enthusiasm and creativity.

For several years I was mass media consultant to Family Counseling & Guidance Centers which was headed by Monsignor Alves. They had a network of clinics in Boston and suburban areas.

Considering the awful impact my mother's insanity had on my life, it was good for me to work with people dedicated to improving people's mental health.

During my years with the agency, we were pioneers in providing public awareness for the problem of mood swings people often had after the Christmas Holidays. Year after year I stimulated substantial media coverage on the post-Holiday blahs and blues as well as other psychological problems that coincided with seasons or holidays.

Since God works in mysterious and fascinating ways, I also became a communications consultant to the central office of Catholic Charities serving Greater Boston. Life had taken me from childhood in a Catholic Charities group home to consultant for the agency overseeing the Catholic Charities in eastern Massachusetts.

Feeling a bit like a character in a Dickens novel with a secret origin, it was heartwarming for me to learn of the sincere dedication of the Catholic Charities staff to the well-being of the people they served.

My work with the central office of Catholic Charities led to other consulting opportunities with Catholic Charities agencies in Cambridge and north and south of Boston.

My years as an independent consultant with large and small agencies provided me with a continuing education in the world of health and human services. Those years also gave me many challenges in working with all kinds of people trying to serve others.

During my years of working with nonprofits I had many positive experiences. I enjoyed the work and felt it was a blessing that I was led into a reluctant role as consultant to health and human service agencies. It was the right place for me. My initial reluctance was replaced by enthusiasm.

As I have said before, the Lord functions in fascinating ways. We never can be absolutely certain of where the Lord is going to take us, but from my perspective it's always interesting. I think of it as a daily adventure.

It's an adventure that makes sense of a Zen expression that I relate to: "Become who you are."

It is my belief that deep inside each of us there is a hidden potential waiting to be tapped. For some of us, that potential is so hidden that we can fail to see it. For others we may know it's there but think that we are not destined to access it.

Even though I had my family history to assist my awareness, it was easy to overlook the lessons that came down to me from my father and my grandfather.

My grandfather had run away from home at age 14 and developed the skills to become an excellent barber. This led to a life of self-employment in his shop in the days when a barbershop was a lively center of community activity.

It took my father almost to middle age before he had the courage to break loose from the U.S. Postal Service and escape to Maine where he would become an entrepreneur with Brookland Motor Court in Wells, Maine.

I broke loose and became a freelance misfit at age 46.

Chapter 16
Family Life

Life as a freelance writer and consultant is not without stress, as I have already noted. Neither is family life which can erupt in great distress. As 1980 opened, my marital distress reached a challenging level.

Due to differences that had become more and more irreconcilable I had made a decision to do something that had always terrified me. To understand myself better I entered psychoanalysis with a Jungian analyst who had been trained in Zurich at the Jung Institute. This experience was a catalyst for major changes in my life.

Brookline psychoanalyst Joel Covitz and I were able to analyze dreams and discuss realities of my emotional life such as the impact of my mother's insanity and my Catholic Charities orphan experience. I had never shared these facts with anybody else. I still use some of his advice and I repeat his actual words when faced with difficult decisions.

During this period I also became very moderate about my use of alcohol. It seemed that I was benefiting greatly from the nine months of Jungian psychoanalysis. But major changes were imminent.

Finally, early in 1981 my marital separation after 27 years of marriage began. We had developed serious differences that could not be reconciled. For me, the separation and eventual divorce led to intense loneliness, staggering financial challenges, slow adjustment to solitary living, and growth of new self-respect based on love of self and others.

At the time of the separation, my three daughters were young adults, but my son was only ten. He and I were very close and it was extremely difficult to be away from him and my young adult daughters on a day-to-day basis.

The pain of divorce seemed almost unbearable at times, but we all lived through it and grew emotionally. For me, it was my road less traveled. This was the road less traveled that poet Robert Frost and writer Scott Peck had referred to.

In a state of deep mourning I lined up on my bureau all the available photos of people I had loved and lost as well as pictures of myself in my early years. Then I prayed about the losses and cried a flood of tears and screamed primal screams. It was one of the most difficult periods of my life.

I moved into a period of rapid downward mobility after the divorce and within a few years I was entirely without property. I had gone from being a potential real estate millionaire to being a pauper. I lost real estate wealth but I gained greatly in spiritual development.

During this unsettling period, I was destined to roam like a modern day gypsy from apartment to apartment in Dedham, Canton, and on Cape Cod for more than fifteen years. That was an adventure in its own right. Finally, thanks to a continuation of my G.I. Bill of Rights I became eligible to have my own house again here on the Cape in 1998.

As I leave my five-room writing cave on Cape Cod and drive out my driveway each day, if I turn my head to the right I see the salt pond at the end of my street and the sand dunes, beach house, and lifeguard station in the distance.

I could not ask for a better location and I have no complaints about the ups and downs I have experienced as a divorced Dad or as a freelance writer, author, lecturer, educator and communications consultant. I see it all as part of God's plan for the unfolding of my journey through life.

I see God as the author of my life story but in the chapters he gives me free will to make my own decisions. This grateful orphan thanks God daily for the life story God has written. For me, it has been a very interesting journey.

Chapter 17
Freelance Writing and TV Production

My life as a freelance writer motivated me to accept my friend Will Solimene's urging that I join voluntary associations related to writing. Years before, we had met when I was active in the Publicity Club of Boston. So I followed my friend's advice and became a member of the American Medical Writers Association (AMWA).

Eventually, I was elected President of the New England Chapter and I served on the Board of Directors of the national organization. Around this time, I also became President of Professional Writers of Cape Cod.

As an active member of AMWA, I attended conferences in various U.S. and Canadian cities. Prior to a conference in Toronto I was asked to present a session titled, "Launching a Freelance Writing Career." Based on that presentation I was invited later to write a chapter on the same subject for the AMWA book *Biomedical Communication.*

For many years I had been a featured guest on just about every major radio and TV discussion show in the Boston and Eastern Massachusetts areas. Because I had felt comfortable as a guest the thought of having my own show entered my mind and motivated me to make a proposal.

After conceiving the public affairs show "It's Your Life," I visited a few media outlets with my package and got a show of interest in the Boston suburb of Needham at Channel 25 WXNE-TV. Soon I was the host of my own public affairs show on Channel 25 when it was owned by the Christian Broadcasting Network.

After I got the green light, we were launched based on this statement: "We'll try it for thirteen weeks." We produced two shows at a time twice a month and my show

"It's Your Life" ran on Channel 25 every Sunday evening for nearly three years.

At the end of each show, as I was signing off I said, "Thank God for making this show possible." This was based on my belief that anything I do is only possible because of my Creator's decision to grant me the life I have lived.

During my early years of freelancing I was led by my intuition to North Shore Council on Alcoholism, other councils on alcoholism, and Boston's Third Nail Drug Program. So I began to specialize in writing about addiction.

I view the addictions as our world's major health problem leading to serious diseases of mind, body and spirit. I believe addictions are the idols that get between us and our Creator.

But there is another way to look at our addictions. I found it in the writing of William Blake the poet and mystic. "The road of excess leads to the Palace of Wisdom." Pain and suffering lead to recovery and health. The addict who finds recovery becomes enlightened and approaches life in a less self-centered way. Helping others leads to happiness.

In 1983 I was visiting my professional lobbyist friend Tom Driscoll who was handling public affairs for Mount Pleasant Hospital, an addiction treatment center in Lynn, Mass. He gave me a copy of *The U.S. Journal of Drug & Alcohol Dependence* and said they seldom included information from the Northeast.

Tom suggested that I offer to be a freelance correspondent for the *Journal* in New England. I followed his advice and that fall they tested me with the assignment of covering a conference on alcoholism at Newport, Rhode Island.

I was soon their National Correspondent in the northeast, covering addiction conferences and writing feature articles each month to inform health professionals. I served in this capacity for eight years and I loved it.

Chapter 18
International Correspondent

On many occasions, my freelance writing combined work with pleasure. In 1984, one of these life-changing occasions was when I followed a suggestion by my mentor Mark Keller, a pioneer in the alcoholism field. Editor Emeritus of Rutgers’ Journal of Alcohol Studies, Mark was a colleague of mine in the American Medical Writers Association.

Based on Mark’s insistent prodding, I went to Israel for that nation’s first International Conference on Alcoholism and the Family. Shimon Peres, Labor Minister, spoke at the opening. Attendees came from around the world.

Before the conference I spent time in Italy. In Rome I received special treatment at the U.S. Embassy because former Governor of Massachusetts John Volpe contacted the Ambassador in Rome about me. An Italian interpreter was assigned to me so I could do addiction related interviews at government agencies and addiction treatment centers.

Before returning home after the conference in Israel I spent time in Egypt, an astounding mystical experience. Later I did travel writing about Italy, Israel and Egypt.

Another example of combining business and pleasure was my 1985 trip to the University of Stirling at Edinburgh, Scotland. This was a special assignment from the Rev. David Works. I covered a conference stimulated by his North Conway Institute, an addiction ministry located in Boston.

The conference was about alcoholism in the workplace and was hosted by the Church of Scotland. In addition to the writing I did for the North Conway Institute, I was able to write about that Scottish conference for the *U.S. Journal of Drug and Alcohol Dependence*.

While attending the conference in Scotland I met a health

professional from Sweden who surprised me by telling me he was familiar with my writing in the *U.S. Journal*. We writers don't know how far our words will travel. Feedback is rare.

Before returning home, I made my first visit to Ireland where I interviewed experts and gathered additional material for freelance articles on Irish alcoholism.

As time passed, I wrote for such publications as *The Journal* of the Addiction Research Foundation in Toronto and the *Medical Post*, another Canadian publication.

In *Catholic Digest* I wrote feature stories on the lives of Boston's Cardinal Medeiros and "The Junkie Priest," Father Dan Egan, who was not a junkie himself but helped many drug addicts. I interviewed him at the Graymoor monastery in upstate New York near the Hudson River.

Working in the addiction field led me to take a close look at my own use of alcohol and valium. Therefore, I decided in 1983 to abstain from alcohol and other drugs. It was a healthy decision. Since then I have not found it necessary to consume mind altering substances. That has left my mind free for God to do any altering that needed to be done.

I have had a varied set of experiences during this time on Earth that we call "life." Through God's grace I have had many dreams come true, in workplaces and other places. Nevertheless, the most amazing event in my life was not directly related to work. It related to my spiritual journey.

In spiritual development, the ability to endure and then enjoy solitude is very important. As I look back on my life, I can see that it was necessary for me to spend long periods living alone during the years leading to my spiritual enlightenment at Peterborough, New Hampshire, in the Monadnock Mountains on September 5, 1985.

I encourage you to get a copy of *The Monadnock Revelations: A Spiritual Memoir* which provides the details of my journey. Also, you may ask me to send you a detailed summary of how I channeled the voice of God. Contact me at P.O. Box 25, Dennisport, MA 02639. The summary is free but please send me $5. for postage and handling.

Since September 5, 1985 I have been leading somewhat of a double life as a man who has experienced God directly through "Cosmic Consciousness" and a person pursuing an apparently ordinary life as a freelance writer, professional lecturer, and educator. It's an enjoyable adventure.

The hour I spent in the dazzling Light of the Presence of God provided answers to every question I ever had about my life and what it was all about. Since that day at the age of 53 my life as an orphan has made sense to me. And I was told by God that even our Creator feels like an orphan at times.

I was informed that God loves all people unconditionally whether they believe in God or not. It was revealed to me that Jesus is indeed the Beloved Son of God and will soon return to our planet as it was explained in the Scriptures.

I was told to practice meditation the way the Lord guided me into that Benedictine practice. And I was told to tell others to practice silent meditation. So do it! Do it every day!

Of the messages that God delivered to me on September 5, 1985 in the Monadnock Mountains, please remember this one: "I love them. Tell them how much I love them." Everyone is included in God's Love. No exceptions.

God is not a myth. Jesus is not a myth. They are more real than what we call reality. I have seen and heard Jesus and I have experienced the Light and Voice of the Heavenly Father (The God of Love). I wish everybody could have such experiences. They change the way a person looks at life.

My own belief in what I cannot usually see is more real to me than the daily reality my senses present to me. I believe I am a spirit residing temporarily in this body. And I believe that is true of all of us. I have had proof of this, directly from the Source. Believe what I have said here. It is God's truth.

Chapter 19
The Freelance Writer on Cape Cod

Shortly after my astounding spiritual experience on September 5, 1985, I moved to Cape Cod. I had a few Boston area clients when I moved here. Then I rapidly attracted an arrangement with Monomoy Community Services, a mental health agency headquartered in Chatham. That agency was my first Cape Cod client. I soon got more.

Was I in my element as a freelance writer on Cape Cod? Yes. I had made the right decision when I parted company with the Massachusetts Safety Council on Flag Day, June 14, 1978, my last day of full-time employment.

After arriving on Cape Cod on Columbus Day, 1985, I continued my affiliation with the Cape Cod Writers' Conference which later evolved into the Cape Cod Writers' Center. I served on the Board of Directors and was part-time Program Director for the Center for a year or so. I had the pleasure of introducing humorist Art Buchwald who was featured speaker at the Annual Conference.

Before moving to the Cape I had been the only off-Cape member of a group called The Twelve O'Clock Scholars. During one of these meetings another member suggested that I utilize my writing at *The U.S. Journal of Drug and Alcohol Dependence* and adapt it to some local writing on the Cape.

So I made a proposal to the *Cape Cod Times* about doing a weekly column on the addictions. By the time January 1986 arrived I was writing a weekly column, "On Addiction." It appeared every Thursday in the *Times* on the Advice page in an excellent spot next to Ann Landers.

The editor, Bill Breisky, had said, "Do four columns and we'll try it for a month and see how it goes." For the next thirteen years my column appeared each Thursday, reaching between 50,000 and in excess of 100,000 readers, depending on how many visitors were in the area. So I had an audience for my insights into addiction and spirituality.

Bill Breisky told me that my column was one of his favorites. However, a while after he retired, the new editor who replaced Bill at the *Cape Cod Times* dropped my column. C'est la vie. "Freelance" doesn't mean "permanent."

I was able to continue the addiction theme for a while in a health/lifestyle column for the *Cape Cod Journal*, the first online daily newspaper in America, which advertised that it was "ahead of the *Times*." I guess it was too far ahead. It went out of business due to a dearth of advertising revenue.

Concentrating on TV production as a member of Cape Cod Community Media Center, I produced more than twenty 30-minute videos with the title "Understanding Addiction." Essentially, this was a condensation of the information in my book *Addicted? A Guide to Understanding Addiction.*

Continuing my addiction theme, I wrote my addiction column once a month for five years in *The Cape Codder*. In the end, I had written newspaper columns on the Cape for 20 years when I called it a day. Since then I have concentrated on lecturing and publishing my books.

One of the aspects of my addiction writing that I treasure is the ability to discuss spirituality. Addiction is physical, mental, emotional, social and spiritual. But from my perspective, spirituality is at the heart of the matter.

Alcoholics Anonymous and other Twelve Step programs are essentially spiritual. And the spiritual journey is very relevant to addiction recovery.

After all, the addictions that afflict us are what I consider to be the idol worship that has always been a challenge for the human condition in the battle between good and evil, the struggle between the Light and the darkness.

Chapter 20
Freelance Writer and Professor

For years after teaching Psychology and Philosophy courses at New Hampshire College while in Maine, the idea of doing more college level teaching hovered in the back of my mind. When I was settled on Cape Cod for a while I filed an employment application at our local Community College.

In the fall of 1988 I became an adjunct English Professor at Cape Cod Community College, a member of the faculty in the Language and Literature Department. An "adjunct" is a part-timer who has to sign a separate contract for each semester's assignment. A professional "temp."

During this period, in addition to teaching one or two writing courses, I developed a community services course about addiction based on my book *Addicted? A Guide to Understanding Addiction.* Later, I provided a course in healthy relating which is so important in addiction recovery. That course was based on my book *Improving Intimacy: 10 Powerful Strategies~A Spiritual Approach.*

Not long after arriving on Cape Cod I was fortunate to attract a client that kept me busy for several years. At Beech Hill Hospital in Dublin, New Hampshire, a pioneering addiction treatment facility, I served as their communications consultant and handled their mass media needs. Also, I was Editor of their "News" publication that circulated to many thousands of Beech Hill alumni and a large number of professionals in the addiction field nationwide.

It was an ideal freelance assignment with an excellent hourly rate and the pleasure of doing my writing and editing at my home office in Dennisport on Cape Cod where I sat at my TRS-80 ("Trash 80") computer/word processor in a rented condo with an ocean view of Nantucket Sound.

I handled interviews of Beech Hill staff by phone and on-site during monthly visits to the hospital atop a small mountain in the Monadnock area at Dublin, New Hampshire.

The assignment with Beech Hill lasted until the national recession of 1990-1991 during which the health care sector was hit very hard. Also, I was hit with great impact. More than half my monthly income came from that facility.

On a wintry visit to Beech Hill I was invited into Vice President Sally Morgan's office where I heard a comment I will always remember: "Tom, we're going to have to curtail your activities after you complete your current work."

The following months brought perilous downward mobility. Since Beech Hill had provided more than half of my income, I could no longer meet my obligations. I only had a few small clients and was nearly flat broke.

After going through all the red tape that the welfare system entails, I was told that my monthly income was 100 dollars too high to qualify for food stamps. This was one among many frustrating experiences in that recession.

No matter where I turned, work eluded me. No longer did I have the situation where I would leave one job on a Friday and start a new one the following Monday. I was blocked.

Because I had no desire to become a full-time Professor, it was with some reluctance that I began teaching additional courses at Cape Cod Community College. Soon, by necessity, I was carrying almost a full-time load of three English courses plus some community service courses.

This began to feel like the kind of full-time work I had become allergic to. So it was a challenging time for this orphan, especially with my low threshold for stress.

As for stress, during my freelance years I was better off when it came to stress. But I still had an exquisitely sensitive nervous system that had accompanied me since infancy. So I had to pace myself. Sometimes I was good at pacing myself;

other times I was not. I tended to be inconsistent.

When I taught two sections of the same course I would find myself repeating the same joke to a class, handing out Xeroxes I had already given them, or commenting on an assignment I had already covered.

In my own way, I was becoming an absent-minded professor. I had never been adept at repetitive functions. I preferred the variety that makes life interesting.

In 1991, to add to my income and my stress I also took on a 20-hours-a-week job at the College as a writing coach, mentor, and academic advisor for occupational education students. When I joined the part-time staff of Carol Dubay's Coaches & Mentors Program, I had to reduce the number of English courses I was teaching.

Both the part-time teaching position plus the tutoring and advising for the Coaches & Mentors Program were destined to run for about 20 years. But I didn't think this conflicted with my pledge never to stay in the same full-time occupation more than five years.

After all, I was part-time faculty, not full-time. And the tutoring/advising role was part of a Federal grant program that could be ended just about any time.

Serving Cape Cod Community College was a useful and gratifying way for me to stay afloat financially. I met many fine people during those years of teaching and tutoring. And I have many excellent memories from that part of my life.

To this day, when I take a walk at the Cape Cod Mall in Hyannis, I often meet former students. In fact, yesterday a student near a store called out to me and reminded me of the seminar he attended in which I presented information on how to write a research paper. He said he was very grateful.

And that made my day.

Chapter 21
Lectures, Books and Social Security

With the passage of time and advancing senior citizen status, I moved away from communications consulting and concentrated on my own writing while teaching and tutoring writing at Cape Cod Community College.

In recent years I have left my work in higher education at the Community College. I have gradually adjusted to being a basically "retired" person. I survive financially mostly due to the Social Security retirement system.

This lifestyle puts me "on the edge" of society. But I can meet my basic needs for food, clothing, and shelter. And I have the time to write my books. So I have no complaint.

After all, I believe God led me to this way of functioning and I choose to accept God's will for me. Actually, it fits in nicely with my Franciscan outlook in which various kinds of relative poverty are spiritual virtues. My writing has turned out to be truly not-for-profit. But that's okay.

Before I had my Cosmic Consciousness experience on September 5, 1985, I was a bit irritated with God for choosing to give me the difficult kind of life experiences that I have encountered. But now, as this book's title suggests, you may just "Call Me An Orphan." I'm okay with that.

If some people don't understand me and what makes me tick, it's no big deal. An orphan like me is a misfit, so I can't be fully understood by so-called "normal" people. Also, at times I am pretty much of a mystery to myself. That's the way it is. And that's the way the Lord arranged it.

Hey, I am an orphan and have known no other kind of life. So that's what I am. It was not easy to be an orphan, especially the odd kind of orphan with two living parents; one insane and the other an escape artist.

I was in denial about being an orphan for a long time. But it's my role given to me by the Lord. So I accept my role as a misfit on this strange planet. That's my part in the divine drama and it's up to me to play that part as well as I can.

Early in this book I provided a look at the Lahey Clinic's investigation into my dramatic reactions to the stress in my life. As I come near the end of this memoir I think it's a good time to look again at that information, especially the results of the Minnesota Multiphasic Personality Inventory (MMPI).

During May 1976 at Boston's world renowned Lahey Clinic when I was 44 years old, my attending physician and a staff psychiatrist used the MMPI to try to understand my possibly "psychosomatic" physical disturbances and my mental tendency toward some anxiety and depression.

The following gives you a few highlights from my MMPI results:

- Highly rebellious and nonconformist
- Touchy, sensitive
- Artistic, bohemian temperament
- Confused feelings, moody
- Moderately depressed, worrying
- Restless or agitated

The words "Posttraumatic Stress Disorder" were not included when the situation was explained to me. The initials PTSD were seldom used in those days. But obviously, a person with my MMPI test results could now easily be viewed as a candidate for the PTSD diagnosis.

When I first read my medical file and found the MMPI results, I thought they had exaggerated. But now, as I have reviewed my life in this memoir I don't find much of a problem with the report. After all, the results of the MMPI were based on my honest answers to the questions.

I have experienced periodic horrendous stress from the

very first days of my long orphan/misfit life. Naturally, PTSD is part of the game of life for me. It was good that I learned how PTSD is a factor to one degree or another in a wide variety of mental health and nervous system disorders.

PTSD needs much more attention individually and throughout society. It has been a very important factor in my personal development and will continue to be.

At age 82, have I recovered from the various findings of the MMPI back in 1976? No. Maybe it's part of who I am. Look, I am who I am and there always have been good reasons for the odd "outsider" tendencies of my personality.

It took me a long time to conclude that it's okay to have my particular personal history. But now I say, "What's so bad about my being a misfit? It has made my life interesting and still does." If I am different from the crowd, so what?

As for retirement, I have never believed in that approach as a satisfying way of life. So I did not organize my life in such a way that I would end up well provided for in my senior citizen years. Yet I manage to get by.

When people have asked, "Are you retired?" I sometimes quip, "No, I'm not retired; I'm just tired."

My main focus these days is writing and publishing my own books, a true not-for-profit arrangement due to printing, promotion, and other costs. Also, I do talks for community groups, libraries and others who appreciate my writing.

How do I decide what to do with the parts of my life that I can control to some degree? I turn to my intuition and the guidance of the Lord who has no difficulty communicating to me. In recent years each time I have asked the Lord about choices I should make I have always gotten responses such as "Be useful." So words like those are a good guide.

Years ago, in this age of digital writing and reproduction, I shifted my focus not only to writing my books but also to building my own website. That website has recently been deleted due to an error by the host. I am in the process of building a new one with my name in the domain. I will include many of my essays there on addiction and recovery as a free service for those wishing to learn more about addiction. My website: www.tomoconnellbooks.com

At the end of this book you will find a list of the books I have written and published. My books are available through any bookseller. The author/publisher: Tom O'Connell.

Also, if you are on a tight budget, just send five bucks for postage to me at Box 25, Dennisport MA 02639 and enclose whatever you can afford for a book. I'll mail you a book.

I am grateful to the following booksellers on Cape Cod: Booksmith/Musicsmith in Orleans, Books by the Sea in Osterville, Market Street Books at Mashpee Commons, and the Keltic Kottage in West Yarmouth.

As a public service, I am producing a series on Cape Cod's public access Channel 99 highlighting my published books. It is called "Books, Etcetera with Tom O'Connell."

It's a showcase for my books and as time goes by it will provide a way for me to do commentaries on my other writings. On some shows I have guest book reviewer Allan Cole asking me questions. On other shows I go solo.

Also, I will soon have most of my books available at Amazon and on Kindle.

In an attempt to lead a fairly balanced life I maintain my affiliations with New England Chapter of the American Medical Writers Association, A Book in the Hand, Irish American Club of Cape Cod, Boston College Alumni Association, and Boston University Alumni Network.

I am a member of Cape Cod Community Media Center and I am marginally involved with Cape Cod Writers Center. In addition, I am a member of the Roman Catholic Church and a Secular Franciscan. Also, I attend Twelve Step "anonymous" mutual help groups that help me deal with my obsessive-compulsive tendencies. I meditate daily.

As I look back on my life in this 12th book I can clearly see how lucky I have been through the years to find useful work while being part of a loving family, relating to an abundance of good friends and colleagues, and pursuing creative goals near and dear to my heart.

On my journey through life some very pleasant surprises have come my way. One was *Cape Cod Life Magazine's* selection of me in their 25th Anniversary issue as "one of the top 100 influential people" on Cape Cod. This exaggeration was pleasant because I did not seek this recognition.

As I have noted before, everything else in my life pales before the gift of spiritual enlightenment and Cosmic Consciousness the Lord gave me in a direct encounter on September 5, 1985. It was a supremely special hour.

So I have no need to complain about most of the challenges that life poses for this misfit. However, I do complain sometimes. I am not a saint and I am very sensitive to various kinds of pain. But God is okay with my whining. At the end of each day I thank God for every event I have experienced whether or not I have appreciated it.

The Lord chose the dramatic role of misfit for me on the stage of life. And it has been a challenging role to play. But what would life be without challenges? I view the challenges as part of God's will for me. I trust God's plan for my life.

After all, decades ago I chose to be "in the world but not of the world" when I elected to be guided by the lives of Jesus the Christ ("I am the Way") and Francis of Assisi ("Forget yourself" and "Expect nothing"). Did I choose a life without obstacles? A life without sacrifice? An easy life?

I believe some of the hardest parts of my journey have been about forgiveness. Jesus provided the supreme example when he was experiencing excruciating pain on the cross and said, "Forgive them; they know not what they do."

In this memoir I have aimed more attention at my father's shortcomings than I intended to. But even though his impact on my life was often painful, he could be generous as well. Basically, I had a deep spiritual need to forgive him for the ways he abandoned and neglected me. I did forgive him.

From my early years I was aware of his own suffering based on the loss of my mother and my brother. So I had compassion for my father and the pain that life had inflicted on him. As much as I may have hated the decisions he made about my life, I avoided condemning him as a person.

Looking back, I think his dedication to his second family in Maine must have offset the neglect I received from him. He was a reliable father for the six children in that family.

When I was an adult he apologized to me for the life I had to live because he was unavailable. He said he was amazed I did not turn out to be some kind of destructive public enemy.

Periodically, over the years he came to my aid in many ways. As I have noted earlier, he could be generous from time to time. For example, he might provide a new stove or refrigerator or an old car when my growing family needed one. I appreciated that kind of generosity.

Eventually, on September 5, 1985 at Mount Monadnock when the Light of God came to me and the voice of God filled my emptiness, my life experiences were clarified when the Lord said these words: "I have given everything in your life to you to prepare you to be my prophet." It became clear that my primary role in life is to be a messenger of the Lord.

It is obvious to me that the hand of God has been involved in every moment of my orphan life by direct intervention or God's permission. Life itself has been an ongoing gift for this grateful orphan. I have been very blessed.

What a journey life is. What an adventure. What a piece of work. I wish you joy in your own "work" and fulfillment in your journey through life. May God bless you.

About the Author

The 25th Anniversary issue of *Cape Cod Life Magazine* selected Tom as "one of the top 100 influential people" on Cape Cod. Also, he is listed in *Who's Who in the East.*

Tom is a Cape Cod Writer and Lecturer. Take a look at his new website where you will find many essays as well as excerpts from his books. Go to www.tomoconnellbooks.com

A Few Facts

Bachelor of Arts *cum laude.* History & Government.
Boston College, College of Arts & Sciences.
Also, advanced Graduate Study at Boston College.

Master of Arts. History. (U.S. and European).
Boston University,
Graduate School of Arts & Sciences.

Served as Dedham (Mass.) School Committee Chairman, Town Meeting Member, Statewide Political Campaign Organizer, Lobbyist at State House, Beacon Hill, Boston.

Formerly the CEO of four different organizations: Chevrolet Dealers Association, Boston Public Housing Tenants Policy Council, Massachusetts Federation of Nursing Homes, Massachusetts Safety Council.

Independent Freelance Writer & Editor since 1978.

Publisher, *Lifestyle Journal.*

His website provides excerpts from twelve books and lifestyle essays emphasizing addiction and recovery.

Past President, American Medical Writers Association, New England Chapter. Member (1980-).

English Professor, Adjunct Faculty,
Cape Cod Community College (1988-2007).

Writing Tutor/Mentor/Advisor,
Cape Cod Community College (1991-2010).

Member, Cape Cod Writers' Center (1981-2013).
Served as Board member and Program Planner.

National Correspondent, *U.S. Journal of Drug & Alcohol Dependence* (1983-1991).

Columnist, *Cape Cod Times* (1986-1999).

Columnist, *Cape Cod Journal* (1999-2000).

Columnist, *The Cape Codder* (2000-2005).

Affiliated with A Book in the Hand at Sears Library.

Served as Political Commentator, campaign2america.com

Member, Secular Franciscan Order (1980-)

Tom O'Connell Books
PO Box 25, Dennisport, MAssachusetts 02639, USA

Call Me An Orphan:
My Life as a Misfit~
A Psychological Memoir
By Tom O'Connell

In a candid, informal style, writer Tom O'Connell traces his life as "a misfit" from his early days in the 1930s and 1940s as an orphan in a Catholic Charities group home upward to top leadership roles in Massachusetts.

In a psychological memoir, he recalls challenging careers as CEO, educator, freelance writer, columnist, host of public affairs show "It's Your Life" on Boston's Channel 25.

The author says, "My point in writing this book is to share with others how it feels to be an orphan, to describe my status as an orphan, and also to relate how being an orphan affected the way I functioned during this long life of mine."

The memoir delivers a roller coaster ride of achievements as he moves up from Granny's duplex next to the railroad tracks to the Governor's Highway Safety Committee, CEO of Massachusetts Safety Council, inclusion in *Who's Who in the East*, and selection in *Cape Cod Life's* 25th Anniversary Issue as "one of the top 100 influential people" on Cape Cod.

O'Connell also tells how he plummeted from the heights into the serious challenges of divorce, illness, bankruptcy.

"Tom's memoirs are written like novels."
--Jordan Rich, *WBZ News Radio* 1030, Boston.
($15)

Upward & Downward Mobility: *A Work Memoir (A Writer's Zigzag Journey)*

In a candid, informal style, writer Tom O'Connell traces his work life from his early days in the 1930s and 1940s as an orphan in a Catholic Charities group home upward to top leadership roles in Massachusetts. He recalls challenging careers as CEO, educator, writer, columnist, host of public affairs show "It's Your Life" on Boston's Channel 25.

People known nationally and locally emerge in this book: Entertainer Victor Borge, Massachusetts Gov. John Volpe, Gov. Mike Dukakis, Newsman Dick Flavin, *Boston Globe* Cartoonist Paul Szep, Gov. Frank Sargent, Boston Mayor Kevin White, Boston City Councillor "Dapper" O'Neil.

The memoir takes the reader on a roller coaster ride of job searches and major achievements as he moves upward from Granny's ancient duplex next to the railroad tracks to member of the Governor's Highway Safety Committee, CEO of Massachusetts Safety Council, inclusion in *Who's Who in the East*, and selection in *Cape Cod Life's* 25th Anniversary Issue as "one of the top 100 influential people" on Cape Cod.

From heights of upward mobility and success, O'Connell also reveals periods when he plummeted from those heights into times of downward mobility when faced with divorce, illness, bankruptcy and other challenges.

"Tom re-creates the 'Anything is Possible' myth of American culture after World War II."

--W. A. Cole, Book Reviewer

"This is more than a lone wolf's professional journal. His long time readers know Tom's independent thinking and deep faith. It's the story of a soul who will not sacrifice his values."

--Dr. Finbarr Corr, Author, Former Priest, Therapist, Professor

($10)

Deviant Shelter:
Year Three of The New Social System (NSS)
A Novel

It is Year Three of The New Social System (NSS) and all mental health institutions, prisons and correctional facilities in the United Econocratic Provinces have been replaced with deviant shelters for those who do not fit the government's current definition of the word "normal."

Doctor Wylie Fayne, a philosophy professor, is the first resident of a new psychological deviant shelter with highly advanced technology. He is housed in a triangular-shaped unit in the Total Scrutiny Wing of the granite shelter constructed as a pyramid.

The professor has the distinction of being the first person to experience the new Time Void Therapy. Neuropsychological implants (NPI) have been attached to his nervous system. The goal of his therapy is to move him toward an acceptable mental condition so he can be useful to the government.

"Engaging…reminiscent of James Joyce, George Orwell, Franz Kafka…unique vision of 21st Century…a dark sense of humor."—W.A. Cole, Book Reviewer. "A vivid imagination…It's so different…I was impressed."—Bob Silverberg, *Books & The World* TV. ($10)

Power, Politics & Propaganda:
Observations of a Curious Contrarian

This collection of thought-provoking essays is a reminder about the importance of individual liberty in a world moving toward more systems of government putting the group first.

O'Connell explores how power, politics and propaganda lead to supremacy of the collective over the free individual.

The danger, he contends, is that despite allegedly good intentions the elite collectivists and secularists are apt to consider those who believe in God as candidates for the Flat Earth Society.

O'Connell's key philosophy: "Individual liberty is our birthright...Respect for life is the key to both individual liberty and group harmony."

He says a Divine Plan is at work in the destinies of individuals and nations. Unimpressed with mob dynamics, he stresses individual liberty.

"You are really pointing the pathway here."--Bob Silverberg, *Books & The World* TV. "I thoroughly enjoyed your eye opening and thought-provoking book…It's a great read."—Jack Coffey, retired entrepreneur. "O'Connell's book is political prophecy."—W.A. Cole, Book Reviewer. ($10)

Bugging Out: An Army Memoir (1954)

With wit and irony, the author uses candid dialogue and vivid descriptions to tell how he dealt with the military assaults on his independent personality.

As a "voluntary" draftee with a pregnant wife, he is demoralized by cruel superiors and caught between duty and self-preservation. Reluctantly, he turns to "bugging out" as he tries to cope with the Army's challenges to his sanity.

His memoir provides memories of his adventures as a military misfit. Scenes reflect outrage, despair, and hilarity.

"Very vivid...a fascinating read."—Bob Silverberg, *Books & The World* TV. "A real picture of what it was like...no holds barred."--*Provincetown Banner.* "A let-it-all-hang-out memoir...interesting characters."-*Barnstable Patriot.* ($10)

The O'Connell Boy: Educating "The Wolf Child" ~ An Irish-American Memoir (1932-1950)

Lively impressions of a "wolf child" life in homes with solitary Irish immigrant women. Nine years at Mrs. White's "lace curtain Irish" Catholic Charities group home with her perfectionist "reign of terror." Then a "free" teen's "battle of wits" with Irish Granny on "the other side of the tracks."

"Tom O'Connell connects with readers soul to soul...inspires."--Jordan Rich, *WBZ News Radio* 1030, Boston. "a page-turner...heart wrenching...stunning."--*Cape Cod Magazine.* "a fascinating memoir...a charming and honest writing voice."--*The Cape Codder.* "O'Connell writes compellingly..."--*Cape Cod Times.* "compelling and inspiring."--*Barnstable Patriot.* ($10)

Improving Intimacy: 10 Powerful Strategies ~A Spiritual Approach

A look at spiritually based intimacy, addictive relating, control, listening, communication, conflict. 10 strategies for healthy, loving relationships.

"Positive...powerful...very readable style."--*Cape Cod Times.* "It's the finest example of anyone writing on this subject."--Don LaTulippe, WPLM, Plymouth. ($10)

The Odd Duck: A Story for Odd People of All Ages

A cheerful, inspiring fable for "adult children." A lost duck raised in a chicken coop feels odd. After an identity crisis, a quest for self-worth brings healthy, lasting love.

"A cheerful, punning little allegory mostly for grownups."--*Bostonia Magazine.* "a parable for spiritual reawakening."--*Seniors Cape Cod Forum.* ($10)

Danny The Prophet: A Fantastic Adventure

A man reluctant to be God's last prophet has more worldly plans. A fantastic journey: a politician, a sage, an angel, many perilous adventures, divine revelations.

Readers' say: "Astounding!" "Wow!" "Funny!" "A wonderful book!" "A pleasure to read!" ($10)

Your comments on this book will be much appreciated!

Tom O'Connell Books www.tomoconnellbooks.com
email: irishtommy@comcast.net
PO Box 25, Dennisport, MAssachusetts 02639, USA

www.ingramcontent.com/pod-product-compliance
Lightning Source LLC
Chambersburg PA
CBHW020905090426
42736CB00008B/503
* 9 7 8 0 9 8 2 7 7 6 6 2 9 *